WHAT IS THE STORY OF THE CHURCH?

Kids' Guides to God's Word Series

What Is the Book of Genesis?
What Is the Book of Exodus?
What Is the Book of Leviticus?
What Is the Book of Numbers?
What Is the Book of Deuteronomy?
What Is the Book of Joshua?
What Is the Book of Judges?
What Is the Book of Ruth?
What Is the Book of 1 Samuel?
What Is the Book of 2 Samuel?
What Is the Book of 1 Kings?
What Is the Book of 2 Kings?
What Are the Books of 1–2 Chronicles?
What Are the Books of Ezra & Nehemiah?
What Is the Book of Esther?
What Is the Book of Job?
What Is the Book of Psalms?
What Is the Book of Proverbs?
What Is the Book of Ecclesiastes?
What Are the Books of Song of Songs & Lamentations?
What Is the Book of Isaiah?
What Is the Book of Jeremiah?
What Is the Book of Ezekiel?
What Is the Book of Daniel?
What Are the Books of Hosea–Micah?
What Are the Books of Nahum–Malachi?

What Is the Gospel of Matthew?
What Is the Gospel of Mark?
What Is the Gospel of Luke?
What Is the Gospel of John?
What Is the Book of Acts?
What Is the Book of Romans?
What Is the Book of 1 Corinthians?
What Is the Book of 2 Corinthians?
What Is the Book of Galatians?
What Is the Book of Ephesians?
What Is the Book of Philippians?
What Are the Books of Colossians & Philemon?
What Are the Books of 1–2 Thessalonians?
What Are the Books of 1–2 Timothy & Titus?
What Is the Book of Hebrews?
What Is the Book of James?
What Are the Books of 1–2 Peter & Jude?
What Are the Books of 1-3 John?
What Is the Book of Revelation?

What Is the Story of the
CHURCH?

Michael Whitworth

ISBN 978-1-971767-43-7

Published by Start2Finish
Bend, Oregon 97702
start2finish.org

Printed in the United States of America
30 29 28 27 26   1 2 3 4 5

CONTENTS

INTRODUCTION

Quick quiz. Why are there so many different kinds of churches? Drive through any town in America and you will pass Baptist churches, Methodist churches, Presbyterian churches, Catholic churches, and probably a dozen others. They all read the same Bible. They all claim to follow the same Jesus. So why are there so many of them? Why don't they all just meet together?

And while we are asking questions: Why does the pope exist? Who decided that ministers should wear robes? Where did Christmas traditions come from? Why do some churches baptize babies and others only baptize adults? Why do some churches have organs and choirs and others have rock bands? Why do some churches call their leaders "Father" and others call them "Brother" and others just use first names?

If you have ever wondered about any of that, this book is for you.

Most Christians know the story of Jesus and the early church from the New Testament. And most Christians know what their own church looks like today. But between those two points sits roughly two thousand years of history that almost nobody talks about. It is as if someone handed you the first chapter and the last chapter of a novel and said, "Good luck figuring out the middle."

This book is the middle.

It covers the story of the church from the death of most of the apostles (around AD 70) to the early 1800s, when a group of believers in America began asking a radical question: what if we threw out all the human traditions and simply went back to the Bible? That is roughly eighteen hundred years of drama, and it includes some of the most important events you have probably never heard of.

WHAT YOU ARE ABOUT TO READ

Here is a roadmap of where we are headed.

Chapter One picks up right where the New Testament leaves off. The apostles are dead. The church has to learn to survive without them. You will meet the men who carried the faith forward and discover how the simple, house-church worship of the New Testament began to change almost immediately.

Chapter Two covers nearly 250 years of Roman persecution. Christians were arrested, tortured, burned alive, and thrown to wild animals for refusing to say three words: "Caesar is Lord." You will meet real people who chose death over denial, and you will learn why persecution made the church grow faster, not slower.

Chapter Three tells the story of what happened when the most powerful man on earth became a Christian. Emperor Constantine ended the persecution and showered the church with money, buildings, and political favor. It sounds like a happy ending, but it might have been the most dangerous thing that ever happened to the church.

Chapter Four takes you into the battles over what Christians actually believe. False teachers tried to turn Jesus into something less than God, and the church had to fight back. You will learn how the great councils produced the creeds, how the books of the New Testament were formally recognized, and why getting the identity of Jesus right mattered more than anything else.

Chapter Five follows the church as it splits in two. The Western church, led by the pope in Rome, and the Eastern church, centered in Constantinople, drifted apart over centuries until they formally broke in 1054. You will also learn how monks preserved learning in a crumbling world and how missionaries carried the faith to Vikings, Slavs, and the farthest corners of Europe.

Chapter Six brings you to the medieval church at the height of its power. Popes commanded kings. Armies marched to the Holy Land in the name of Christ. Cathedrals taller than thirty-story buildings rose across Europe. And a barefoot beggar named Francis of Assisi tried to remind the church that Jesus never carried a sword or wore a crown.

Chapter Seven introduces the voices that spoke up before the Reformation. John Wycliffe in England and Jan Hus in Bohemia saw the corruption and said so out loud. One had his bones dug up and burned. The other was burned alive. But their ideas refused to die.

Chapter Eight is about Martin Luther and the moment that split Western Christianity wide open. A troubled monk discovers that salvation is a gift, not a paycheck, and the most powerful institution in Europe will never be the same.

Chapter Nine follows the Reformation as it ripples outward. John Calvin builds the foundation of Presbyterianism. Henry VIII breaks with Rome for reasons that have nothing to do with theology. The Anabaptists push further than any other group and get persecuted by everyone. And the Catholic Church fights back. By the end of the chapter, the one church has become many.

Chapter Ten crosses the Atlantic. Different denominations claim different colonies. Quakers settle Pennsylvania. Congregationalists build New England. John Wesley's Methodists ride horseback into the frontier. The Great Awakenings sweep the nation with waves of revival. America separates church and state for the first time in Western history. And in the midst of all that diversity, a growing number of believers start asking the question that will give birth to the Restoration Movement: what if we just went back to the Bible and nothing else?

WHY THIS MATTERS

You might be thinking, "That is a lot of history. Why should I care about stuff that happened hundreds of years ago?"

Because you are living in the middle of it. The church you attend, the way you worship, the Bible you hold in your hands, the freedom you have to believe whatever your conscience tells you—none of that dropped out of the sky. Every bit of it was shaped by the decisions, the debates, the courage, and the failures of Christians who came before you.

Understanding their story helps you understand your own. It helps you see why the church drifted from the New Testament pattern and how that drift happened: not in one dramatic moment but in hundreds of small, gradual steps over many centuries. And it helps you appreciate the men and women who gave everything they had to pull the church back toward the truth.

More than anything, this story will remind you that the Bible is enough. Every problem the church has faced over the past two thousand years can be traced back to the same mistake: adding human traditions to God's word. Every recovery has come from the same solution: going back to what the Bible actually says. That pattern repeats itself in every century, on every continent, in every generation.

Including yours.

BEFORE YOU START

A few things to keep in mind as you read.

The story moves through a lot of time. This book covers eighteen centuries. Some chapters span hundreds of years. We can't cover everything, so we will focus on the turning points: the moments when the church changed direction in ways that still affect us today.

The history gets messy. The story of the church is not a neat, clean progression from good to better. It includes corruption, violence, betrayal, and failure alongside courage, faithfulness, and sacrifice. The Bible does not sugarcoat the failures of God's people, and neither does this book. But even in the darkest chapters, God is at work.

This points somewhere. Every chapter in this book is heading toward the same conclusion: the Bible contains everything the church needs. No pope, no creed, no human tradition can improve on what God has already revealed. The call to go back to the New Testament is not a call to live in the past. It is a call to build the future on the only foundation that will last.

The apostle Paul wrote that there is "one body and one Spirit, one Lord, one faith, one baptism" (Ephesians 4:4–5). This book is the story of how that one faith became many, and why a growing number of believers decided it was time to make it one again.

The story begins on the day the last apostle closed his eyes for the final time and the church had to figure out how to keep going without him.

Turn the page.

1

AFTER THE APOSTLES

Thirteen-year-old Brian Robeson is stranded in the Canadian wilderness. His pilot has died of a heart attack, the small plane has crashed into a lake, and Brian is completely alone. No phone, no map, no adult to tell him what to do next. All he has is the hatchet his mother gave him before the trip. In Gary Paulsen's novel *Hatchet*, Brian must figure out how to build shelter, find food, make fire, and survive day after day with no one to guide him. The people who had always taken care of him are gone. Everything he learned from them is still inside his head, but now he has to put it into practice on his own.

The early church faced something like Brian's situation. For roughly forty years after Jesus rose from the dead, the apostles had been there. They were eyewitnesses of Jesus' life, death, and resurrection. They had walked with him, eaten with him, and heard his teaching straight from his lips. When questions came up about what Christians should believe or how churches should be organized, the apostles could settle the matter. They wrote letters that circled among the churches. They traveled from city to city, preaching and teaching and correcting problems. They were the living link between Jesus and his followers.

But by the end of the first century, that link was gone. One by one, the apostles died. James was executed by King Herod. Paul was likely beheaded in Rome. Peter, according to early tradition, was crucified upside down. John, the last surviving apostle, died near the end of the first century. The generation that had known Jesus personally was passing from the scene.

So what happened next? Did the church fall apart? Did it lose its way? Or did it find a path forward? The answer to those questions fills the rest of this book. But this chapter focuses on the very first stretch of that journey: the years between roughly AD 70 and AD 150, when the church had to learn how to stand on its own.

A WORLD ON FIRE

The year AD 70 was a turning point for both Jews and Christians. That year, the Roman army marched into Jerusalem and destroyed the Jewish temple. The temple had stood at the heart of Jewish life for centuries. It was the place where sacrifices were offered, where priests served, and where God's presence was said to dwell. When the Romans burned it to the ground, an entire way of life collapsed along with it.

For Christians, the destruction of the temple confirmed something Jesus himself had predicted (Matthew 24:1–2). But it also meant that the old world they had known was disappearing. Christianity had been born in the soil of Judaism, and many of the first believers were Jewish. Now that soil had been scorched. The church would have to grow in new directions.

And grow it did. By the end of the first century, churches could be found scattered across the Roman Empire: in modern-day Turkey, Greece, Italy, Egypt, and North Africa. Some of these churches had been planted by Paul or other apostles. Others had been started by ordinary believers who carried the gospel with them as they traveled for work or fled from persecution. Christianity was not a movement that depended on a single leader or a single city. It was spreading like seed carried on the wind.

THE MEN WHO CAME NEXT

When the apostles died, leadership of the church did not disappear. It passed to a new generation of men who had known the apostles personally or had been trained by them. Historians often call these men the "apostolic fathers" because they were so closely connected to the apostles themselves. Three of them stand out.

Clement of Rome was a leader in the church at Rome near the end of the first century. Around AD 96, he wrote a letter to the church in Corinth. That church was having problems (just as it had when Paul wrote to them decades earlier). Some younger members had pushed out the church's established leaders, and the congregation was in an uproar. Clement's letter urged them to restore order, to practice humility, and to remember that God is a God of order, not chaos. What makes Clement's letter so interesting is what it tells us about the early church. Even after the apostles were gone, churches were still writing to each other, still correcting each other, and still trying to follow the pattern the apostles had laid down.

Ignatius of Antioch was a church leader in Syria. Around AD 110–115, he was arrested by the Roman authorities and sent to Rome to be executed. On his journey to Rome, he wrote seven letters to various churches. These letters are passionate, urgent, and deeply personal. Ignatius knew he was going to die, and he wanted to use his last days to strengthen the churches he loved. He wrote about the importance of unity, the reality of Jesus' humanity (against those who claimed Jesus only appeared to have a body), and the courage it takes to remain faithful under pressure. Ignatius is one of the earliest examples of a Christian leader who saw his coming death not as a defeat but as an opportunity to honor Christ.

Polycarp of Smyrna had been taught by the apostle John himself. He served as a leader of the church in Smyrna (in modern-day Turkey) for decades. Late in his life, around AD 155, the Roman authorities arrested him and demanded that he deny Christ. According to the account of his death, Polycarp replied, "Eighty-six years I have served him, and he has done me no wrong. How can I blaspheme my King who saved me?" He was burned at the stake. Polycarp's long life bridged two eras. He had known an apostle face to face, and he died as a witness to Christ in a world where all the apostles were long gone.

These three men show us something important. The church after the apostles was not leaderless. God raised up faithful men who carried the message forward. But these men did not claim to be apostles. They did not write new Scripture. They saw themselves as servants whose job was to guard and pass along the teaching the apostles had already delivered.

HOW THE EARLY CHURCH WORSHIPED

What did a church gathering look like in the early second century? It was probably simpler than most people imagine. There were no church buildings yet. Christians met in private homes, sometimes in rented halls, and occasionally in outdoor spaces. There were no stained-glass windows, no organs, and no choirs in matching robes.

An early Christian document called *The Teaching of the Twelve Apostles* gives us one of the earliest glimpses of Christian worship outside the New Testament. Written sometime in the late first or early second century, it describes how early Christians practiced baptism, observed the Lord's Supper, prayed, and fasted. The instructions are remarkably simple. Baptism was to be done in the name of the Father, Son, and Holy Spirit, with flowing water preferred. The Lord's Supper was observed with prayers of thanksgiving. Christians were expected to pray regularly and to live honest, generous lives.

Other early writings confirm this picture. When Christians gathered on the first day of the week, they sang hymns, read from the writings of the apostles and the Old Testament, heard a message from one of the church's leaders, prayed together, and shared the Lord's Supper. Offerings were collected to help the poor, widows, and orphans. There was no elaborate ritual. Worship centered on the word of God, prayer, and fellowship.

This simplicity is worth noticing because, as we will see in later chapters, worship practices gradually became more complex over the centuries. Ceremonies, rituals, and traditions were added layer by layer until the simple gatherings of the New Testament church looked very different from the ornate services of later centuries. But at the beginning, the church worshiped in a way that would have been recognizable to anyone who had read the book of Acts.

ORGANIZING FOR THE LONG HAUL

The apostles had given the churches a basic structure. Each congregation was led by elders (also called shepherds or overseers) and served by deacons. This pattern shows up clearly in the New Testament. Paul told Titus to "appoint elders in every town" (Titus 1:5), and he described the qualities these leaders should have.

After the apostles died, this structure continued. But over time, changes began to creep in. One of the most significant changes was the rise of a single leader in each congregation who held more authority than the other elders. Ignatius' letters, for example, speak of "the bishop" as a single leader who oversees the elders and deacons beneath him. Ignatius was describing something that had developed after the deaths of the apostles (and was not practiced in the book of Acts). By the middle of the second century, many churches were being led by a single overseer, or bishop, rather than by a group of elders who shared authority equally.

This shift happened gradually, and it happened for understandable reasons. When false teachers threatened a congregation, it was easier for one recognized leader to speak with authority than for a committee to debate. When persecution came, churches needed decisive leadership. But the long-term consequences of this change were enormous. The simple, shared leadership of the New Testament slowly gave way to a more centralized system. Over the centuries, this trend would eventually produce the office of the pope. The seeds of that development were planted in this very early period.

A FAITH WORTH DYING FOR

One of the most remarkable things about the church in this period is that it grew even though being a Christian could get you killed. Rome did not launch a full-scale, organized persecution against Christians during these earliest decades, but local outbreaks of hostility were common. Christians were viewed with suspicion. They refused to worship the Roman gods. They refused to offer incense to the emperor. They met in private, which led to wild rumors about what they were really doing behind closed doors.

Despite all of this, the church continued to spread. New believers kept coming. Why? Partly because the message of the gospel was compelling on its own terms: forgiveness of sins, the hope of resurrection, and a God who loved ordinary people. Partly because the way Christians lived their lives attracted attention. They cared for the sick. They took in abandoned children. They shared their resources with the poor. They treated each other as family across ethnic and social lines. In a world where life was often brutal and cheap, Christians offered something different.

The Roman Empire was vast, wealthy, and powerful. The church was small, poor, and had no political influence. Yet within a few generations, Christianity had spread to every corner of the empire. No army carried it. No government funded it. It traveled by word of mouth, by the example of changed lives, and by the courage of men and women who believed that Jesus was worth living for and, if necessary, dying for.

STANDING ON THEIR OWN

Back in *Hatchet*, Brian eventually learns to survive. He makes mistakes. He eats the wrong berries and gets sick. He struggles to build a fire. But slowly, painfully, he figures it out. The lessons his mother and his teachers had given him were not wasted. They came back to him when he needed them most.

The church after the apostles went through something similar. The apostles were gone, but their teaching was not. Their letters were copied, circulated, and read aloud in churches across the Roman world. The truths they had taught were repeated, defended, and passed to the next generation. The church made mistakes along the way. Some of those mistakes would grow into serious problems in the centuries ahead. But in this early period, the church proved that it could stand on its own, not because it was strong enough in itself, but because the one who had promised "I will build my church" (Matthew 16:18) was still at work.

The apostles had planted the seeds. Now a new generation would tend the garden.

WHAT THIS MEANS FOR US

First, every generation must take ownership of its faith. The apostles could not believe for the next generation, and neither can our parents or grandparents. Each of us must decide for ourselves to follow Jesus and to learn his word. The early church survived because ordinary Christians took the faith seriously and made it their own.

Second, simple worship is powerful worship. The earliest churches did not need elaborate buildings, professional musicians, or complicated ceremonies. They needed the word of God, prayer, the Lord's Supper, and hearts devoted to Christ. We should never confuse fancy with faithful.

Third, good leadership matters. The apostolic fathers show us that churches need godly, humble leaders who guard the truth and serve the people. When leadership goes wrong, the effects can be felt for generations. When leadership goes right, the church stays strong even under pressure.

Fourth, how we live preaches louder than what we say. The early church grew not only because of its message but because of its lifestyle. Christians who care for the poor, love their neighbors, and live with integrity will always make an impression on the world around them.

TALKING POINTS

1. **Brian in Hatchet had to survive without the people who had always guided him.** What are some things you have learned from parents, teachers, or mentors that you might need to rely on someday when they are not around?

2. **Clement, Ignatius, and Polycarp each served the church in different ways.** Which of the three do you find most interesting, and why?

3. **Early Christians worshiped in simple ways: reading Scripture, praying, singing, and sharing the Lord's Supper.** How does that compare to what you see in churches today? What do you think are the most important parts of worship?

4. **The Roman Empire tolerated many different religions, but Christianity made the authorities uneasy.** Why do you think the Roman Empire was suspicious of Christians? What made Christianity so different from the religions Rome was used to?

5. **Polycarp said, "Eighty-six years I have served him, and he has done me no wrong."** What does that statement tell you about the kind of relationship Polycarp had with Jesus? What would it take for you to have that kind of faith?

The church had learned to stand on its own after the apostles. It had faithful leaders, a simple pattern of worship, and a message that was changing lives across the Roman Empire. But standing on your own is one thing. Standing your ground when the most powerful empire on earth decides to crush you is something else entirely.

The scattered, local hostility that Christians had faced so far was about to become something far worse. Emperors would issue orders to hunt down believers, burn their Scriptures, and force them to deny their faith or die. The next chapter of the church's story is written in blood.

Turn the page.

2

THE BLOOD OF THE MARTYRS

Stanley Yelnats did not steal the sneakers. But that did not matter. In the 2003 film *Holes*, based on the novel by Louis Sachar, Stanley is wrongly convicted of theft and sentenced to Camp Green Lake, a brutal juvenile detention center in the Texas desert. There is no lake. There is no shade. Every day, the boys must dig a hole five feet deep and five feet wide in the scorching sun. The warden is cruel, the guards are heartless, and the whole system is designed to grind the boys down until they stop asking questions. Stanley is punished for something he did not do, and there is nothing he can do about it except endure.

For the first three centuries of its existence, the church found itself in a similar position. Christians had not committed any crime. They were not planning to overthrow the government. They were not dangerous. But the Roman Empire treated them as though they were all of those things. Over the course of roughly 250 years, Christians were arrested, tortured, thrown to wild animals, and burned alive—not because of what they had done, but because of who they were and what they refused to do. This chapter tells the story of how the church survived the worst the most powerful empire on earth could throw at it.

WHY DID ROME CARE?

To understand why Rome persecuted Christians, you need to understand how religion worked in the Roman world. Rome was remarkably tolerant of other religions. When the Roman army conquered a new territory, it usually let the people keep worshiping their own gods. Rome did not care which gods you prayed to, as long as you also showed loyalty to the emperor.

That loyalty was expressed through a simple act: burning a pinch of incense at a temple and saying the words, "Caesar is Lord." It was not really about religion. It was a political loyalty test, like saluting a flag. After you did it, you received a certificate proving your loyalty, and then you could go worship any god you liked. Most people in the empire had no problem with this. Their local gods did not mind sharing space with the emperor.

But Christians could not do it. For a follower of Jesus, there was only one Lord, and it was not Caesar. Saying "Caesar is Lord" was not just an empty phrase to them. It was a denial of the most basic truth of their faith: that Jesus Christ alone is Lord over all. They would pray for the emperor, but they would not pray *to* him. To the Romans, this looked like stubbornness at best and treason at worst.

There were other reasons for Roman suspicion too. Christians refused to worship the traditional Roman gods, and many ordinary Romans believed this made the gods angry. When earthquakes, plagues, or famines struck, it was easy to blame the Christians. "The gods are punishing us because these people refuse to honor them!" was a common cry. Christians also kept to themselves socially. They could not attend many public events because those events involved sacrifices to pagan gods. They would not watch the gladiatorial games where men killed each other for entertainment. They seemed withdrawn, secretive, and strange.

Because Christians met in private homes and spoke of "eating the body" and "drinking the blood" of their Lord (referring to the Lord's Supper), wild rumors spread about them. Some Romans accused them of cannibalism. Others suspected them of immoral behavior behind closed doors. These rumors were completely false, but they gave the public one more reason to fear and hate the Christian movement.

THE FIRST FIRES

The earliest official persecution of Christians came from the emperor Nero in AD 64. A massive fire broke out in Rome that summer, raging for six days and damaging or destroying ten of the city's fourteen districts. Rumors spread that Nero himself had started the fire. Whether that was true or not, Nero needed someone to blame, and he chose the Christians. They were already unpopular, they were an easy target, and they had no powerful friends to protect them.

The punishments were horrifying. Some Christians were covered in animal skins and torn apart by dogs. Others were crucified. Still others were coated in pitch and set on fire to light Nero's gardens at night. According to early tradition, both Paul and Peter died during this persecution. Paul was beheaded (as a Roman citizen, he was given that "privilege"), and Peter was crucified upside down.

Nero's persecution was important because it set a pattern, even though it was limited to the city of Rome and did not target Christians specifically for their beliefs. It showed that the empire could turn against Christians whenever it was convenient. The door to persecution had been opened.

A POLICY TAKES SHAPE

For the next few decades, persecution was scattered and unpredictable. The emperor Domitian (AD 81–96) enforced emperor worship and punished those who refused, including Christians. But it was during the reign of Trajan (AD 98–117) that Rome developed its first official policy on how to handle Christians.

A Roman governor named Pliny was stationed in the provinces of Bithynia and Pontus in modern-day Turkey. He noticed that Christianity was spreading rapidly in his territory. Pagan temples were emptying out. Meat sacrificed to idols was going unsold. Pliny was not sure what to do, so he wrote a letter to Emperor Trajan asking for guidance.

Pliny explained his current approach: he would ask an accused person three times whether they were a Christian, each time threatening punishment. If they still said yes after the third question, he had them executed. Trajan wrote back with an official policy: Christians were not to be hunted down. Anonymous accusations were not to be accepted. But if someone was formally accused and convicted of being a Christian, and they refused to worship the Roman gods, they were to be punished.

This policy might sound almost fair, but it created a terrible situation. Being a Christian was now officially a punishable offense. Your survival depended on whether your neighbors liked you enough to leave you alone. If someone had a grudge against you, all they had to do was report you, and you faced a choice: deny Christ or die.

WHEN THE EMPIRE STRUCK WITH FULL FORCE

For most of the first two centuries, persecution was local, not empire-wide. One province might be dangerous for Christians while another was relatively safe. But in the middle of the third century, things changed dramatically.

The emperor Decius (AD 249–251) believed that Rome's troubles (military threats, economic collapse, plagues) were caused by the anger of the old gods. He decided that every person in the empire must come before a government official, offer a sacrifice to the gods, and receive a certificate proving they had done so. This was not aimed specifically at Christians, but it flushed them out. Anyone who refused to sacrifice was identified as disloyal and punished severely.

The Decian persecution hit the church hard. Church leaders were arrested first, leaving congregations without guidance. Many Christians who had never been seriously tested in their faith gave in and offered the sacrifice. But many others refused and paid with their lives or their freedom. Some were executed. Others were sent to work in mines and quarries, half-starved, chained, and beaten daily. These believers faced what one historian called "a living death." After about a year, the persecution faded, and Decius himself died in battle. But the church had been shaken.

The worst was yet to come. In AD 303, the emperor Diocletian launched the most severe and systematic persecution in the church's history. He issued a series of orders: Christian meeting places were to be destroyed, Scriptures were to be burned, clergy were to be imprisoned, and all Christians were to sacrifice to the pagan gods or face death. In the eastern part of the empire, the persecution was especially brutal. Christians were tortured, mutilated, and killed in large numbers.

But not everyone cooperated with Diocletian's orders. In the western provinces, a co-ruler named Constantius refused to execute anyone for their faith. He destroyed a few church buildings to keep up appearances, but he would not shed blood. His son would later change the course of Christian history. His name was Constantine.

FACES IN THE FIRE

Numbers and dates can make persecution feel distant and abstract. But behind every statistic was a real person with a real name who made a real choice. A few of their stories have survived.

Justin was a philosopher who converted to Christianity after years of searching for truth in Greek philosophy. He opened a school in Rome and wrote some of the earliest and most important defenses of the Christian faith. Around AD 165, during the reign of Marcus Aurelius, Justin and six of his students were arrested. The Roman judge ordered them to sacrifice to the gods. Justin refused. "Do what you will," he told the judge. "We are Christians, and we do not sacrifice to idols." Justin and his companions were scourged and beheaded. He has been known ever since as Justin Martyr.

Perpetua was a young noblewoman in North Africa, about twenty-two years old and the mother of an infant son. She was arrested around AD 203 along with her slave Felicity, who was pregnant at the time. Perpetua's father begged her to deny her faith, not because he hated Christianity, but because he loved his daughter and could not bear to see her die. Perpetua refused. According to the account of her imprisonment, she told her father, "I cannot call myself by any other name than what I am: a Christian." Both Perpetua and Felicity were executed in the arena at Carthage. Their courage made such an impression that their story was read aloud in churches for generations.

These were not unusual cases. Across the empire, ordinary men and women faced the same terrible choice. A mother, a student, a craftsman, a slave—any of them might be called to account for their faith on any given day. What is remarkable is how many of them chose death over denial.

WHY THE CHURCH GREW ANYWAY

Here is the great paradox of this period: the more Rome tried to stamp out Christianity, the more it spread. Persecution did not kill the church. In many ways, it made the church stronger.

The courage of the martyrs made an impression on people who watched them die. When a Christian walked calmly into an arena and refused to beg for mercy, even Roman spectators sometimes asked themselves, "What do these people have that I do not?" The early Christian writer Tertullian captured this when he wrote that "the blood of the martyrs is the seed of the church." Every execution planted questions in the minds of those who witnessed it.

Persecution also forced Christians to scatter, and as they scattered, they carried the gospel to places it had never been. Like dandelion seeds blown by a strong wind, believers landed in new communities and started new churches. What Rome meant to destroy, God used to spread.

The experience of suffering also helped settle an important question: which writings were truly Scripture? Under persecution, Christians would not risk their lives to protect a document unless they believed it was the genuine word of God. The books they copied, hid, and died for were the ones the church recognized as the New Testament.

But persecution had its darker effects too. Not every Christian stood firm. Some denied their faith under pressure and then wanted to come back to the church after the danger passed. This created painful arguments. Should they be welcomed back? Some churches said yes. Others said no. The question of the "lapsed" divided congregations and caused wounds that took years to heal.

THE FIRE GOES OUT

By the early fourth century, it was clear that persecution had failed. After Diocletian stepped down from power in AD 305, the empire fell into a period of confusion and civil war. Out of that chaos rose Constantine, the son of the one ruler who had refused to shed Christian blood. What Constantine did next would change everything, not only for the church, but for the entire Roman world.

The era of the martyrs was ending. But the lessons it taught still echo across the centuries. Christ had warned his followers,

"If they persecuted me, they will also persecute you" (John 15:20). For 250 years, those words had proven painfully true. And for 250 years, the church had answered with a faith that fire could not consume.

WHAT THIS MEANS FOR US

First, faith will be tested. The early Christians did not face persecution because they were doing something wrong. They faced it because they were doing something right. Following Jesus has never been a guarantee of comfort, and there will be times when standing for the truth costs something.

Second, Christ is the only Lord. The early Christians could have saved their lives with a single sentence: "Caesar is Lord." But they knew that only Jesus deserves that title. We face our own versions of that test every day, whenever the world pressures us to put something else above our loyalty to Christ.

Third, suffering can produce growth. This is not a reason to seek out suffering, but it is a reminder that God can use even the worst circumstances to accomplish his purposes. The church grew under persecution because God was at work in ways no emperor could control.

Fourth, courage is contagious. The bravery of the martyrs inspired others to believe. When we stand firm in our faith, even in small ways, it encourages the people around us to do the same.

TALKING POINTS

1. **Stanley in Holes was punished for something he did not do, and he had to decide whether to give up or keep**

going. The early Christians were in a similar spot. What do you think gave them the strength to endure?

2. **The Romans saw saying "Caesar is Lord" as a harmless political gesture, but Christians saw it as a denial of their faith.** Can you think of situations today where something seems small on the surface but actually involves a bigger principle?

3. **Perpetua's father begged her to deny Christ, not out of cruelty but out of love.** How would you respond if someone you loved asked you to give up your faith for your own safety?

4. **Tertullian wrote that "the blood of the martyrs is the seed of the church." The more the Romans persecuted Christians, the faster the church grew.** Why do you think opposition and hardship sometimes make a movement stronger instead of weaker?

5. **Not every Christian stood firm under persecution. Some denied their faith and later wanted to come back.** If you had been part of an early church, would you have welcomed them back? Why or why not?

The age of the martyrs had proven that no human power could destroy the church. But what would happen when the power that had been trying to crush Christianity suddenly decided to embrace it? The next chapter of the church's story is not about an emperor with a sword. It is about an emperor with a cross on his shield, and the surprising dangers that came with his friendship.

Turn the page.

3

THE EMPEROR'S NEW FAITH

Picture this. You and a handful of friends have been running a small club at school. Maybe it started as a service project or a Bible study. You meet in someone's garage after school. You bring your own snacks. You sit on folding chairs. The group is small, but everyone is there because they genuinely care about the mission. Nobody joins for popularity points. Nobody even knows the club exists except the people in it.

Then one day, everything changes. The principal hears about your group and decides to make it an official school organization. A wealthy parent offers to sponsor it. Suddenly you have a real room, a budget, matching T-shirts, and a spot in the school newsletter. Kids who never gave your group a second look are lining up to join.

At first, it feels like a dream come true. But slowly, things start to shift. The sponsor has opinions about how the meetings should run. The new members do not care about the mission the way the original group did. Some of them are only there because it looks good on a college application. The meetings get bigger and fancier, but the heart of the group feels different.

You got everything you thought you wanted, and it is quietly changing who you are.

That is almost exactly what happened to the church in the fourth century. After nearly 250 years of persecution, the most powerful man in the world suddenly became a Christian. And the church would never be the same.

THE MAN BEHIND THE CROSS

His name was Constantine, and his rise to power reads like a movie script. His father, Constantius, had been one of four co-rulers of the Roman Empire. Constantius was the one ruler during the Diocletian persecution who refused to execute Christians. When Constantius died in AD 306, his soldiers immediately declared Constantine the new ruler of their portion of the empire. But Constantine was not the only man who wanted to be emperor. Several rivals stood in his way.

The most important showdown came in AD 312 at the Milvian Bridge, just outside Rome. Constantine was marching south to face his rival Maxentius, whose army was larger and better positioned. According to the church historian Eusebius, Constantine saw a vision in the sky before the battle: a cross of light with the words, "In this sign, conquer." That night, Constantine reportedly had a dream in which Christ told him to put the symbol of the cross on his soldiers' shields.

Whether the vision was genuine or not, Constantine obeyed. His soldiers painted the Christian symbol on their shields, marched into battle, and won a decisive victory. Maxentius drowned in the Tiber River while trying to retreat. Constantine entered Rome as the undisputed ruler of the western empire, and he credited his victory to the God of the Christians.

THE DOORS SWING OPEN

The very next year, in AD 313, Constantine and his eastern co-ruler Licinius issued what is known as the Edict of Milan. This decree gave full legal toleration to Christianity throughout the Roman Empire. It was no longer a crime to be a Christian.

But Constantine went far beyond mere toleration. He returned property that had been seized from Christians during the persecutions. He funded the construction of grand new church buildings, including the original Church of the Holy Sepulcher in Jerusalem and the Church of the Nativity in Bethlehem. He exempted Christian ministers from military service and from paying certain taxes. He gave church leaders an honored place at his court. By AD 324, when Constantine became the sole ruler of the entire empire, Christianity had gone from being an outlawed movement to the emperor's favorite religion in barely a decade.

For believers who had lived through the nightmare of Diocletian's persecution, this must have felt like a miracle. Churches that had been torn down were being rebuilt, bigger and grander than before. Scriptures that had been burned were being copied again by the thousands. Preachers who had been hiding in basements were now dining with government officials. The historian Eusebius, who lived through this era, compared Constantine's victory to the parting of the Red Sea. It seemed like God himself had intervened to rescue his people.

THE PRICE OF POWER

But miracles can be complicated. Along with all the genuine blessings came a set of problems that nobody had anticipated.

The first problem was the flood of new converts. When being a Christian could get you killed, only people with genuine faith joined the church. Now that being a Christian could get you a promotion, the church filled with people who had very different motives. Government officials, military officers, and ambitious politicians flocked to the faith because the emperor favored it. Many of these newcomers had little understanding of the gospel and even less interest in living by it. They brought their pagan habits, superstitions, and attitudes right through the church doors.

The second problem was political interference. Constantine saw himself not only as the emperor but as a kind of overseer of the church. He called church councils, weighed in on theological debates, and expected church leaders to obey his decisions the way his generals obeyed his military orders. When disputes arose among Christians, Constantine treated them as political problems to be solved by imperial authority. The church had gained a powerful protector, but that protector expected to have a say in how things were run.

The third problem was subtler but perhaps the most dangerous of all. As the church grew wealthier and more influential, it began to look and feel more like the empire it served. Simple meeting places gave way to enormous, ornate buildings modeled on Roman government halls. Worship services—once plain and focused on Scripture, prayer, and the Lord's Supper—became increasingly elaborate ceremonies with special robes, processions, and rituals borrowed from the imperial court. The ministers who had once been servants among equals began to look more like Roman officials, complete with titles and ranks and political influence.

None of this happened overnight. It crept in gradually, one change at a time, each one seeming harmless on its own. But over the course of a century, the church that emerged looked very different from the one described in the book of Acts.

FROM TOLERATED TO REQUIRED

If Constantine opened the door, the emperor Theodosius kicked it off its hinges. In AD 380, Theodosius declared Christianity the official religion of the Roman Empire. His decree left no room for ambiguity. He commanded that all citizens "shall practice that religion which the divine Peter the Apostle transmitted to the Romans." Anyone who refused was labeled "demented and insane" and threatened with punishment.

By AD 392, Theodosius had gone further still, banning pagan worship altogether under severe penalties. The tables had completely turned. Christianity had once been the persecuted religion. Now it was the persecuting religion. Pagan temples were closed, sometimes destroyed. People who had once forced Christians to sacrifice to Roman gods now found themselves being forced to abandon those same gods.

This was a breathtaking reversal, and it raised a troubling question. Jesus had never forced anyone to follow him. He invited people. He persuaded them. He loved them. But he never used the power of the government to compel belief. Now his followers were doing exactly that, and many thoughtful Christians were deeply uneasy about it.

DID THE CHURCH WIN, OR DID IT LOSE?

One of the sharpest observations about this period comes from the historian Howard Vos: "It seems unwise to speak of the church's conquering the Roman Empire. One might as easily argue that the empire had conquered the church."

That sentence is worth reading twice. On the surface, the church had won. Christianity was no longer hiding in homes and catacombs. It was the official faith of the most powerful empire on earth. But beneath the surface, something essential had been lost. The line between the church and the world had become dangerously blurred.

Before Constantine, the church was small, poor, and pure. You joined because you believed, and you stayed because your faith was real, even if it cost you everything. After Constantine, the church was large, wealthy, and mixed. Genuine believers sat next to people who had been baptized for political reasons and who still privately worshiped the old gods. The church had traded its simplicity for splendor, its independence for imperial favor, and its purity for numbers.

This does not mean that everything about the Constantinian era was bad. The end of persecution was a genuine blessing. The freedom to worship openly, to build churches, to copy and distribute Scripture without fear was an enormous gift. Many sincere Christians used this new freedom to do great good. But the alliance between church and state introduced problems that would haunt Christianity for more than a thousand years, and some of those problems still echo in churches today.

WHAT CHANGED IN WORSHIP

One of the most visible changes during this period was in how Christians worshiped. In the New Testament and in the earliest centuries, worship was simple. Christians gathered on the first day of the week in homes or small meeting places. They sang, prayed, read Scripture, heard teaching, and shared the Lord's Supper. Leadership was provided by a group of elders who served as shepherds of the congregation.

Under the influence of the empire, worship gradually became more formal and ceremonial. Church buildings were designed to impress, with high ceilings, marble columns, and elaborate decorations. Ministers began wearing special garments to set them apart. Incense, candles, and processions were added to services. The Lord's Supper, once a simple shared meal of remembrance, became an increasingly mysterious ritual performed by clergy while the congregation watched.

Some of these changes were borrowed directly from the imperial court. Just as subjects approached the emperor with elaborate ceremony, Christians now approached worship with similar pomp. Others were adapted from the very pagan practices Christianity had replaced. As one historian noted, paganism infiltrated the church in "numerous subtle ways," carried in by the crowds of half-converted newcomers who brought their old religious instincts with them.

The simple, Scripture-centered worship of the early church was slowly buried under layers of tradition and ceremony. It would take more than a thousand years, and a movement called the Reformation, before anyone seriously tried to dig it back out.

THE EMPIRE FALLS, THE CHURCH REMAINS

There is one more twist to this chapter of the story. The Roman Empire that had adopted Christianity did not last. In AD 476, the last Roman emperor in the West was overthrown by Germanic invaders. The mighty empire that had persecuted the church, then embraced the church, and finally tried to control the church crumbled into dust.

But the church did not crumble with it. Christianity survived the fall of Rome and continued to spread among the very peoples who had brought the empire down. The faith proved to be more durable than the government that had tried to make it an instrument of power. That, perhaps, is the most important lesson of this entire era. Empires rise and fall. Christ's church endures.

WHAT THIS MEANS FOR US

First, popularity is not the same as faithfulness. The church looked most impressive when it had the emperor's backing, the biggest buildings, and the largest crowds. But it was arguably most faithful when it was small, simple, and sincere. We should never measure the health of a church by its size or its influence.

Second, power changes people. When the church gained political power, it began to act like a political institution. Christians who had once been persecuted for their faith started persecuting others. Power is a dangerous tool, and it can corrupt even well-meaning people if they are not careful.

Third, simplicity in worship matters. The earliest Christians worshiped in simple ways that put God's word at the center. When the church adopted the ceremonies of the empire, worship became more about spectacle and less about Scripture. Keeping worship simple is not about being boring. It is about keeping the focus where it belongs.

Fourth, the church does not need the government to survive. Constantine's support felt like a rescue, and in some ways it was. But the church had already survived 250 years without any government help. And it outlasted the empire that tried to control it. The church's real strength has never come from political allies. It comes from Christ.

TALKING POINTS

1. **The chapter opened with the image of a small club that changes when it gets a powerful sponsor.** Have you ever been part of a group that changed when it became popular or got outside support? What happened to the original spirit of the group?

2. **Constantine credited his military victory to the God of the Christians. Some people at the time saw this as proof that God was at work. Others have questioned whether Constantine's faith was genuine.** What do you think matters more: why someone says they became a Christian, or how they live afterward?

3. **Before Constantine, only sincere believers joined the church because it was dangerous to be a Christian. Afterward, people joined for political and social reasons.** How can churches today tell the difference between people who are genuinely committed and people who are just going along with the crowd?

4. Emperor Theodosius made Christianity the official religion and outlawed pagan worship. Jesus never forced anyone to follow him. What do you think would have happened if the church had simply kept inviting people to believe and obey Jesus rather than using the government to require it?

5. Howard Vos wrote that "one might as easily argue that the empire had conquered the church." The church gained buildings, money, and political power, but it lost some of its simplicity and purity. Do you think the trade was worth it? Why or why not?

The church had survived persecution and then survived the perhaps more dangerous gift of imperial power. But throughout both eras, questions had been swirling about what Christians actually believed. Who was Jesus, exactly? Was he God, or was he something less? What books belonged in the Bible, and which ones did not? These were not abstract questions for scholars to argue about in libraries. The answers would shape the faith for every generation that followed. The battle for the truth was heating up.

Turn the page.

4

DEFENDING THE TRUTH

Mark Twain's novel *The Prince and the Pauper* tells the story of two boys in sixteenth-century England who look exactly alike. One is Prince Edward, the son of King Henry VIII. The other is Tom Canty, a poor beggar's son from the slums of London. When the two boys meet by accident, they decide to trade places just to see what the other's life is like. But then the switch becomes permanent when the prince is thrown out of the palace and the pauper is mistaken for royalty.

The rest of the book revolves around a single question: who is the real prince? Tom looks the part. He wears the royal robes. He sits on the throne. People bow to him. But none of that makes him the prince. Meanwhile, the real prince is wandering the streets in rags, and almost nobody believes him. Everything depends on getting the identity right. If the wrong boy sits on the throne, the whole kingdom suffers.

The early church faced its own version of this question, and the stakes were even higher. For the first several centuries after Christ, various teachers and movements tried to reshape who Jesus was. Some said he was not really human. Others said he was not really God. Still others stripped away parts of the Bible that did not fit their theories. Each of these groups presented a version of Jesus that looked convincing on the surface but was, in the end, a counterfeit. The church had to fight, sometimes for generations, to get the identity right. Because if you get Jesus wrong, you get everything wrong.

THE GNOSTIC JESUS: A SPIRIT WITHOUT A BODY

The first major threat to the truth came from a movement called Gnosticism, which flourished during the second century. The Gnostics built their belief system on one basic idea: matter is evil and spirit is good. The physical world, including the human body, was a prison for the soul. Salvation meant escaping from the material world and returning to the realm of pure spirit.

This created an enormous problem when it came to Jesus. If matter is evil, then God would never take on a human body. So the Gnostics taught that Jesus only *appeared* to have a physical body. He was a spirit being who looked like a man but was not really one. His birth was an illusion. His suffering on the cross was an illusion. His resurrection was not a bodily event because there was no real body to begin with.

The Gnostics also claimed to have secret knowledge that Jesus had passed down to a select few. This knowledge, not faith in a crucified and risen Savior, was the key to salvation. Only a small, elite group of truly "enlightened" people could be saved. Everyone else was out of luck.

It is hard to overstate how different this was from the faith taught by the apostles. The New Testament is built on the claim that God became flesh (John 1:14), that Jesus physically died on a cross, and that he physically rose from the dead. If the Gnostics had won, the gospel would have been gutted. There would be no real sacrifice for sin, no real resurrection, and no real hope for ordinary people. Christianity would have become a philosophy club for intellectuals rather than good news for the world.

The church fought back. Leaders like Irenaeus and Tertullian wrote detailed arguments against the Gnostics, insisting that the Creator God of the Old Testament and the Father of Jesus were one and the same, that the physical world was good because God made it, and that Jesus was fully and truly human. The early creeds, which we will look at shortly, were written in large part to slam the door on Gnostic ideas.

THE ARIAN JESUS: LESS THAN GOD

If the Gnostics denied that Jesus was truly human, a minister named Arius denied that Jesus was truly God. Around AD 318, Arius, who served a prominent church in Alexandria, Egypt, began teaching that Jesus was not eternal. He argued that Jesus was the first and greatest being that God ever created, but that he was still a created being. "There was a time when the Son did not exist," Arius declared.

To Arius, calling Jesus "God" was an honorary title, not a statement about his nature. Jesus was more than a man but less than God. He was somewhere in between, a kind of divine hero but not the eternal Creator himself.

This teaching was wildly popular. Arius was a gifted communicator who put his ideas into catchy songs and jingles.

Dockworkers, street merchants, and schoolchildren in Alexandria were soon singing his theology on the streets. His ideas also appealed to former pagans who were used to believing in one supreme God surrounded by lesser divine beings. The Arian version of Jesus felt familiar and reasonable to them.

But a young church leader named Athanasius saw the danger immediately. If Jesus is not truly God, then God did not really enter the world to save it. A created being, no matter how powerful, cannot bridge the gap between God and humanity. Only God himself can do that. Athanasius realized that the entire gospel was at stake. If Arius was right, then Jesus was just another creature, and there was no real salvation.

The argument between Arius and Athanasius ripped the church apart. It was not a quiet disagreement among scholars. Riots broke out in the streets of Alexandria. Churches divided. Bishops took sides. The controversy was so intense that the emperor Constantine, who wanted a united church to help hold his empire together, decided to step in.

THE COUNCIL OF NICAEA

In AD 325, Constantine called the first great church council at the city of Nicaea in modern-day Turkey. Roughly three hundred bishops gathered, many of them carrying scars from the recent persecutions. Some had lost eyes. Others had been crippled by torture. These were men who had suffered for their faith, and now they were being asked to define what that faith actually meant.

At the council, supporters of Arius presented their case boldly, arguing that the Son was a created being of a different nature than the Father. The majority of bishops reacted strongly against this. The council ultimately produced a statement of faith known as the Nicene Creed, which declared that Jesus Christ is "true God of true God, begotten, not made, of one substance with the Father." In plain language: Jesus is not a created being. He is fully and completely God, of the same nature as the Father.

Arius and his supporters were condemned. But the controversy did not end with the council. For the next fifty years, the Arian position came back again and again, sometimes with the support of emperors. Athanasius was exiled from his post as bishop of Alexandria five different times for defending the Nicene faith. He earned the nickname "Athanasius against the world" because there were seasons when it seemed like almost everyone in power disagreed with him. But he never backed down.

By AD 381, when a second great council met at Constantinople, the Nicene position had won. The church officially affirmed that Jesus Christ is fully God, equal with the Father, and that the Holy Spirit is also fully God. The doctrine of the Trinity, one God in three persons, was established as the faith of the church.

THE COUNCIL OF CHALCEDON

The Gnostics had denied that Jesus was truly human. Arius had denied that Jesus was truly God. The Council of Nicaea had settled the second question. But a third question still remained: if Jesus is both God and man, how do those two natures relate to each other?

In AD 451, a council met at Chalcedon (near modern-day Istanbul) to address this issue. After intense debate, the council declared that Jesus Christ is one person with two complete natures, fully divine and fully human. These two natures are united in one person without being mixed together, changed, divided, or separated. Jesus is not half God and half man. He is completely both.

This was not an easy idea to put into words. It still is not. But the council recognized that getting it wrong in either direction was far worse than wrestling with mystery. If you lose his humanity, you lose his ability to represent us. If you lose his deity, you lose his ability to save us. The church needed both, and at Chalcedon it said so.

WHICH BOOKS BELONG IN THE BIBLE?

While the church was defining what it believed about Jesus, it was also defining which books carried the authority to shape those beliefs. The New Testament as we know it did not drop from the sky in a leather binding with a table of contents. It took time for the church to formally recognize which books belonged in Scripture and which did not.

This process was driven partly by practical needs. From the very beginning, churches read the apostles' letters and the Gospels aloud in their worship services. But as the decades passed, new writings appeared, some of them claiming to be from apostles who had not actually written them. The Gnostics produced their own "gospels" filled with their secret teachings. A teacher named Marcion created his own shortened Bible by throwing out the entire Old Testament and keeping only parts of Luke and some of Paul's letters. Something had to be done.

The church used several tests to evaluate which books were genuine. The most important was apostolic connection: Was the book written by an apostle, or by someone closely connected to one? Mark was accepted because of his close relationship to Peter. Luke was accepted because of his work with Paul. The church also looked at whether a book's teaching was consistent with what the apostles had taught and whether it had been widely used in churches from early on.

The process took time. Some books, like the four Gospels and Paul's major letters, were recognized almost immediately. Others, like 2 Peter, James, and Jude, were debated for longer. But by AD 367, Athanasius published a list of twenty-seven New Testament books that matches exactly the New Testament we have today. Church councils in North Africa confirmed the same list in AD 393 and 397.

It is important to understand what the church was doing. It was not inventing the Bible. It was recognizing which books God had already inspired. The books did not become Scripture because a council voted on them. They were Scripture because of what they were, and the councils simply acknowledged what the churches had known for generations.

WHY IT ALL MATTERS

All of this might sound like ancient arguments about details that do not affect real life. But consider what was at stake.

If the Gnostics had won, Jesus would have been reduced to a spirit being with no real connection to the physical world. Salvation would be reserved for a tiny elite. The body and the material world would be considered worthless.

If Arius had won, Jesus would have been demoted from God to a powerful creature, and the hope of salvation would have crumbled with him.

If Marcion had won, the Old Testament would have been thrown away and the New Testament would have been sliced down to a fraction of its actual size.

The church fought these battles not because it loved arguing but because it loved the truth. And the truth, once defined, has been the foundation of the Christian faith ever since.

WHAT THIS MEANS FOR US

First, truth matters more than comfort. The false teachings about Jesus were often popular because they were easier to understand or more culturally acceptable. The truth was harder, but the church insisted on it anyway. We should never trade clear biblical teaching for ideas that simply feel more comfortable.

Second, know what you believe and why. The early church was forced to define its beliefs because false teachers were re-defining them. Every Christian should be able to explain the basics of the faith: who Jesus is, what he did, and why it matters. You do not need to be a scholar, but you do need to know the truth well enough to recognize a counterfeit.

Third, the Bible has been tested. The New Testament was not thrown together carelessly. The books in it were carefully recognized over time, tested by their connection to the apostles, their consistency with apostolic teaching, and their use in the churches. We can trust the Bible because it has been through the fire and survived.

Fourth, getting Jesus right is the most important thing. Every major battle in early church history was ultimately about the identity of Jesus. That is because everything else in Christianity depends on who he is. If Jesus is truly God and truly man, then salvation is real, the resurrection is real, and hope is real. If he is anything less, everything else falls apart.

TALKING POINTS

1. **In *The Prince and the Pauper*, the whole kingdom suffered when the wrong boy sat on the throne. The early church believed that getting the identity of Jesus wrong would have similar consequences.** Why do you think it matters so much whether Jesus is truly God and truly human?

2. **The Gnostics taught that the physical world is evil and only the spiritual world is good. The Bible teaches that God created the physical world and called it "very good" (Genesis 1:31).** How does what you believe about the physical world affect how you live your daily life?

3. **Arius put his theology into catchy songs that people sang in the streets. Ideas can spread quickly when they are packaged in an appealing way.** What are some ways that false or misleading ideas spread quickly today, and how can you learn to recognize them?

4. **Athanasius was exiled five times for defending the truth about Jesus. He refused to change his position even when powerful people disagreed with him.** Can you think of a time when you had to stand by what you believed even though it was unpopular? What happened?

5. The church did not invent the Bible; it recognized which books God had already inspired. The tests included apostolic connection, consistency with apostolic teaching, and widespread use in churches. Why do you think these were good tests for determining which books belong in Scripture?

The church had fought to define who Jesus is and which books carry the authority of God's word. Those battles were exhausting, but they gave Christianity a solid foundation of truth. Now the story moves forward in time, as the church faces a different kind of challenge. In the centuries after the Roman Empire split and eventually fell, the church itself began to split. A single bishop in Rome was claiming authority over all other churches, monks were retreating to the wilderness, and the Christian world was slowly dividing into two halves that would one day break apart for good.

Turn the page.

5

TWO ROADS DIVERGE

Maybe it has happened to you, or maybe you have watched it happen to someone you know. Two kids are best friends in elementary school. They do everything together. They sit together at lunch, play together at recess, and spend weekends at each other's houses.

But then middle school comes, and things start to change. One gets really into basketball and starts hanging out with the team. The other joins the school band and spends afternoons in the music room. They do not have a big fight. Nobody slams a door or says something cruel. They just slowly stop having as much in common. The phone calls get shorter. The hangouts get less frequent. And one day they realize they have become two very different people, even though they started out as close as two friends could be.

Something remarkably similar happened to the Christian church. For the first few centuries, believers in the eastern part of the Roman Empire and believers in the western part considered themselves one family. They shared the same faith, the same Scriptures, and the same creeds. But as the centuries passed, the two halves of the church grew up in very different environments. They developed different customs, different languages, different styles of worship, and different ideas about who should be in charge. By the time they realized how far apart they had drifted, it was too late to keep the family together. In 1054, Christendom split in two, and it has remained divided ever since.

This chapter covers the long, slow process by which one church became two. But before we get to the split itself, we need to understand three important developments that shaped the church during these centuries: the rise of the pope, the growth of monasticism, and the spread of Christianity to new peoples.

HOW THE BISHOP OF ROME BECAME THE POPE

In the New Testament, every congregation was led by a group of elders who shared authority equally. There was no single leader over all the churches. But as we saw in Chapter 1, even in the early second century, individual bishops began to gain authority over their congregations. Over time, the bishops of the largest and most important cities gained influence over the smaller churches around them.

No bishop gained more influence than the bishop of Rome. Several factors worked in his favor. First, Rome claimed a connection to the apostle Peter. According to tradition, Peter had served in Rome and been martyred there. Since Jesus had said to Peter, "On this rock I will build my church" (Matthew 16:18), the bishops of Rome argued (incorrectly) that Peter's authority had been passed down to them. This idea, called apostolic succession, became the foundation of papal power.

Second, after the emperor moved the capital of the empire to Constantinople in AD 330, there was a power vacuum in Rome. As the western empire crumbled under invasions from Germanic tribes, the bishop of Rome was often the most stable and powerful figure left in the city. He organized relief for the poor, negotiated with invaders, and sometimes even raised armies. When the political structure collapsed, the church stepped in to fill the gap.

Third, while the eastern church was constantly torn apart by theological controversies, the church in Rome had a reputation for being steady and orthodox. Other churches often looked to Rome for guidance, and this gave the Roman bishop additional prestige.

By the late fifth century, the bishop of Rome was claiming authority not just over the churches in his area, but over all churches everywhere. He adopted the title "pope," from a word meaning "father," and insisted that he was the head of the entire Christian church. Not everyone agreed, especially in the East, where the bishop of Constantinople considered himself equally important. But in the West, the pope's authority grew stronger with each passing century.

GREGORY THE GREAT

No pope did more to establish the power and influence of the office than Gregory I, who served from AD 590–604. Gregory came from a wealthy noble family and had served as the chief civil administrator of Rome before entering the ministry. When he became pope, the western world was falling apart. Germanic tribes had carved up the old Roman Empire into warring kingdoms. Rome itself was plagued by famine, disease, and military threats.

Gregory rose to the challenge. He organized the defense of Rome against the Lombards, a Germanic people who were threatening Italy. He fed the poor, cared for refugees, and managed the church's enormous landholdings to fund charitable work. He was a skilled administrator who turned the office of the pope into a well-organized institution capable of governing not just religious life but civil life as well.

Gregory also had a passion for spreading the gospel. In AD 596, he sent a team of forty monks to England to convert the Anglo-Saxons. Their mission was remarkably successful, and England became one of the most faithful outposts of Roman Christianity.

But Gregory also introduced changes that moved the church further from its New Testament roots. He placed tradition on equal footing with Scripture as a source of authority. He expanded the idea of purgatory, a place where souls were supposedly purified after death. He promoted the practice of praying to saints and the use of relics (objects believed to have belonged to holy people) for spiritual benefit. He transformed the Lord's Supper from a memorial meal into a sacrifice that he said had power over both the living and the dead.

Gregory was a sincere and hardworking leader who genuinely cared about the people he served. But the institution he built looked very little like the church described in the book of Acts. Under Gregory's influence, the medieval papacy took shape, and it would dominate Western Christianity for the next thousand years.

MONKS IN THE WILDERNESS

While popes were building an institution, another movement was pulling Christians in the opposite direction. Monasticism was the practice of withdrawing from ordinary life to devote oneself entirely to prayer, study, and self-discipline.

The roots of monasticism go back to the third and fourth centuries in Egypt. A man named Anthony, inspired by Jesus' words to the rich young ruler ("Go, sell your possessions and give to the poor"), gave away his wealth and moved into the desert to live as a hermit. His example proved contagious. Hundreds of men and women followed him into the wilderness, seeking to escape the distractions of the world and focus entirely on God.

Some of the early monks went to bizarre extremes. They lived in caves, ate nothing but grass, or perched on top of pillars for years at a time. One monk named Simeon Stylites spent over thirty years living on a platform atop a pillar, preaching to the crowds who gathered below.

Over time, monasticism became more organized. A former soldier named Pachomius established the first Christian monastery around AD 320, creating a community where monks lived, worked, and worshiped together under a common set of rules. Later, Benedict of Nursia (around AD 480–547) wrote a famous Rule that became the standard for monastic life in the West. Benedict's monasteries balanced worship, study, and manual labor. Monks recited psalms, copied manuscripts, farmed their land, and served the surrounding communities.

Despite its flaws, monasticism provided some genuine benefits during this period. Monasteries preserved ancient books and learning at a time when much of Western civilization was crumbling. They served as schools, hospitals, and places of refuge. Monks were often the most educated people in their communities, and they played a major role in spreading Christianity to new regions.

But monasticism also reinforced the idea that there were two levels of Christian life: a higher, more spiritual level for monks and clergy, and a lower, ordinary level for everyone else. That distinction has no basis in the New Testament, and it would cause problems for centuries to come.

THE GOSPEL REACHES NEW PEOPLES

Despite its internal struggles, the church continued to expand during this period. Christianity reached peoples and places the apostles never could have imagined.

In the West, missionaries (many of them monks) carried the faith to the Germanic tribes who had overrun the Roman Empire. The conversion of Clovis, a Frankish chieftain, around AD 496 was a turning point. When Clovis became a Roman Catholic Christian, thousands of his warriors followed. The Franks became the most powerful Christian kingdom in Western Europe, and their alliance with the pope would shape European history for centuries.

In the East, missionaries like Cyril and Methodius carried Christianity to the Slavic peoples of Eastern Europe. Cyril is remembered not only as a preacher but as the creator of an alphabet for the Slavic languages, an alphabet still used across much of Eastern Europe and Russia today. In AD 988, the Russian ruler Vladimir was baptized, and Christianity became the faith of the Eastern Slavs.

By the early eleventh century, Christianity had spread to Scandinavia as well. Norway, Sweden, Denmark, Iceland, and even Greenland had embraced the faith. The church that had once been a tiny movement in Palestine now stretched from the frozen north of Europe to the deserts of North Africa, from the British Isles to the borders of India.

A FAMILY DIVIDES

But even as Christianity spread, the family was splitting down the middle. The Eastern church, centered in Constantinople, and the Western church, centered in Rome, had been drifting apart for centuries. By the eleventh century, the differences had become too deep to bridge.

Some of the disagreements were cultural. The West spoke Latin; the East spoke a different language. Western worship used unleavened bread in the Lord's Supper; Eastern worship used leavened bread. Western clergy shaved their faces; Eastern clergy grew beards. Western clergy were required to be unmarried; Eastern clergy were permitted to marry. These differences might seem trivial, but over time they created a sense of strangeness between the two halves of the church. They simply did not recognize each other as family anymore.

Other disagreements were more serious. One involved the question of religious images. The Eastern emperor banned the use of icons (painted images of Jesus and the saints) in worship, while the Western church defended their use. This controversy created a deep rift between Rome and Constantinople that never fully healed.

Another disagreement involved a single word added to the Nicene Creed. The original creed said that the Holy Spirit "proceeds from the Father." The Western church added a phrase meaning "and from the Son." The Eastern church was furious, not only because it disagreed with the theology but because the West had changed the creed without consulting the East.

The deepest disagreement, though, was about authority. The pope in Rome claimed supreme authority over all Christian churches everywhere. The patriarch of Constantinople refused to accept this claim. In the East, the church operated under the authority of the emperor, and the patriarch, while respected, was not independent the way the pope was. Neither side was willing to submit to the other.

THE BREAK OF 1054

The final rupture came in the summer of 1054. Pope Leo IX sent a delegation to Constantinople, led by a man named Cardinal Humbert, to negotiate with the patriarch. The negotiations failed. On July 16, Humbert walked into the great cathedral of Hagia Sophia in Constantinople and placed a document on the altar excommunicating the patriarch and his followers, formally cutting them off from the Western church. The patriarch responded by excommunicating the pope's representatives.

The split was complete. The Western church became known as the Roman Catholic Church, led by the pope. The Eastern church became known as the Eastern Orthodox Church, led by a network of patriarchs. The two halves have never reunited.

The split did not happen because of a single argument. It was the result of centuries of cultural, theological, and political differences that accumulated until the bond finally snapped. Like those two childhood friends who drifted apart without ever having a fight, the two churches had simply grown in different directions for so long that they no longer knew how to be one family.

WHAT THIS MEANS FOR US

First, unity requires constant effort. The Eastern and Western churches did not set out to split. The division happened gradually, one disagreement at a time, over centuries. Unity among Christians does not maintain itself. It requires humility, communication, and a willingness to work through differences rather than letting them fester.

Second, authority must be grounded in Scripture. The rise of the papacy shows what happens when human leadership is given authority that the Bible never granted. The New Testament describes shared leadership among elders, not a single ruler over all churches. When we build systems of authority that go beyond Scripture, we invite the very problems the church experienced.

Third, withdrawing from the world is not the answer. The monks were often sincere and served the church in important ways. But the New Testament does not teach Christians to retreat from society. Jesus prayed for his followers, "I do not ask that you take them out of the world, but that you keep them from the evil one" (John 17:15). Christians are called to live in the world, not escape from it.

Fourth, the gospel crosses every border. During this period, Christianity spread to peoples and cultures the apostles never encountered. The message of Jesus is not tied to any one language, nation, or culture. It is for everyone, everywhere.

TALKING POINTS

1. **This chapter opened with the image of two childhood friends who slowly drift apart without ever having a big fight. The Eastern and Western churches experienced something similar.** What do you think is the biggest reason they drifted apart, and could anything have been done to prevent it?

2. **The bishop of Rome gradually claimed authority over all other churches based on his connection to the apostle Peter. The New Testament shows churches being led by groups of elders, not by one leader over all congregations.** Why do you think the church moved away from the New Testament pattern, and what problems did this create?

3. **Monks like Anthony and Benedict left ordinary life to focus entirely on prayer and devotion to God. Some people admire their dedication while others think Christians should stay engaged with the world around them.** What do you think? Is there value in separating yourself from distractions to focus on God, or is it better to serve God in the middle of everyday life?

4. **Missionaries like Cyril created an entire alphabet so that Slavic peoples could read the Scriptures in their own language. That kind of effort shows how important it was to make God's word accessible to everyone.** What are some ways we can make the Bible more accessible to people around us today?

5. **The split of 1054 came after centuries of small disagreements that were never resolved. Relationships in our own**

lives can break down the same way. Can you think of a time when a small misunderstanding or unresolved tension grew into something bigger? What could have been done differently?

The church was now divided into East and West, and the Western church was firmly under the authority of the pope. In the centuries ahead, that authority would reach its peak. Popes would command armies, launch wars to recapture the Holy Land, and exercise power over kings and emperors. The medieval church would build some of the most magnificent cathedrals the world has ever seen and produce some of its greatest thinkers. But it would also become an institution drunk on its own power, and the cracks in its foundation would eventually bring the whole structure crashing down.

Turn the page.

6

SWORDS AND CATHEDRALS

Emperor Kuzco has it all. In the 2000 animated film *The Emperor's New Groove*, he rules an entire kingdom from a golden palace on a mountaintop. He has servants for everything, a theme song guy who follows him around, and absolute power over every person in the land. And he uses that power exactly the way you would expect a spoiled teenager to use it: selfishly. When Kuzco decides he wants a vacation home with a waterslide, he picks a hilltop that already has a village on it. No problem. He will just knock the village down. The people who live there do not matter. Only the emperor matters.

It takes a long, humiliating journey (including being turned into a llama) before Kuzco begins to see that power is supposed to serve people, not the other way around. Along the way, a humble peasant named Pacha shows him what it looks like to care about others more than yourself.

The medieval church could have used a Pacha. By the twelfth and thirteenth centuries, the pope commanded more power than any king in Europe. The church controlled enormous wealth, built some of the most stunning structures in human history, launched massive military campaigns, and claimed authority over the eternal destiny of every person alive. It was the most powerful institution the Western world had ever seen. But somewhere along the way, the church that Jesus founded to serve the lost and the broken had become an empire that served itself. And one unlikely man from a small Italian town would try to remind it of what it had forgotten.

THE POPE ABOVE ALL KINGS

The papacy reached its peak of power under Pope Innocent III, who served from 1198 to 1216. Innocent was brilliant, well-educated, and utterly convinced that the pope was the supreme authority on earth. He declared that the papacy was like the sun and kings were like the moon: just as the moon has no light of its own but only reflects the sun's, so kings received their authority from the pope.

This was not empty boasting. Innocent had the weapons to back it up. His most feared tool was excommunication, the power to cut a person off from the church entirely. In a world where almost everyone believed that salvation came through the church and its ceremonies, being excommunicated was terrifying. It meant you could not receive communion, your marriage was not recognized, and when you died you would not receive a Christian burial. Peasants, nobles, and even kings trembled at the threat.

If a king defied the pope, Innocent could go further and place an entire country under interdict. This meant that all church services in that nation were suspended. No weddings, no baptisms, no communion for anyone, until the ruler gave in. Innocent used or threatened this weapon dozens of times. When King John of England challenged him, Innocent placed all of England under interdict and excommunicated the king. John eventually surrendered and became the pope's servant, receiving his own kingdom back as a gift from Rome.

The irony is staggering. Jesus had said, "My kingdom is not of this world" (John 18:36). He had washed his disciples' feet. He had told them that the greatest among them must be the servant of all. Now his purported earthly representative was forcing kings to kneel, nations to obey, and entire populations to live in fear of spiritual punishment. The church had become exactly the kind of earthly kingdom Jesus had refused to establish.

THE CRUSADES

Nothing illustrated the church's blending of spiritual authority and military force more dramatically than the Crusades. These were a series of military expeditions launched by the popes to recapture the Holy Land, especially Jerusalem, from Muslim control.

The First Crusade was launched in 1095 when Pope Urban II called on the warriors of Europe to take up the cross and march east. Urban promised that anyone who fought in the Crusade would have their sins forgiven. Thousands responded. Nobles, knights, and common people from across Western Europe set out on the long and dangerous journey. In 1099, after brutal fighting, they captured Jerusalem and set up a string of small kingdoms along the coast of the Middle East.

But the Crusades were far more complicated than a simple story of Christian heroism. The motives of the Crusaders were mixed. Some were driven by genuine religious devotion. Others were looking for adventure, land, or wealth. The behavior of the Crusaders was often horrifying. When they captured Jerusalem, they massacred thousands of the city's Muslim and Jewish inhabitants.

In the Fourth Crusade (1202–1204), the Crusaders never even reached the Holy Land. Instead, they attacked and plundered Constantinople, the capital of the Eastern Christian empire and the home of their fellow believers. The pope, Innocent III, was furious when he heard the news, but he still took advantage of the situation by appointing a Roman Catholic archbishop in the conquered city.

Over the course of two centuries, seven major Crusades were launched. None of them achieved lasting results. By 1291, the last Christian stronghold in the Holy Land had fallen. The Crusades had failed to win the Holy Land permanently, failed to heal the divide between Eastern and Western Christianity (in fact, they made it worse), and left a legacy of violence that continues to shape relations between Christians and Muslims to this day.

The Crusades revealed a fundamental problem. The church had confused the kingdom of God with an earthly empire. It had tried to spread the faith by force, forgetting that Jesus never used a sword to win a single soul. As one historian put it, "the sword is never God's way to extend Christ's church" (see Matthew 26:52).

CATHEDRALS AND UNIVERSITIES

The medieval church did not only build armies. It also built some of the most breathtaking structures in human history. Between

1170 and 1270, more than five hundred great churches and cathedrals were built in the Gothic style in France alone. These soaring buildings—with their pointed arches, stained-glass windows, and towers that reached toward the sky—were designed to fill people with awe and draw their eyes upward toward God.

The Cathedral of Chartres in France stands as tall as a thirty-story building. The Cathedral of Strasbourg reaches forty stories. Walking into one of these spaces, with light streaming through walls of colored glass and the sound of chanting echoing off stone vaults, was meant to feel like stepping into heaven itself. The cathedrals were the greatest artistic achievement of the Middle Ages, and they remain among the most impressive buildings ever constructed.

The church also gave birth to the first universities. Schools attached to cathedrals and monasteries gradually developed into independent institutions of learning. The University of Paris, the University of Bologna, and the University of Oxford all trace their origins to the twelfth and thirteenth centuries. These universities produced brilliant thinkers who wrestled with questions about God, creation, and the nature of truth. Thomas Aquinas, the most famous scholar of the era, wrote massive works of theology that attempted to combine Christian faith with the philosophy of the ancient world.

The cathedrals and universities show that the medieval church was not all corruption and power politics. It was also a place of genuine beauty, learning, and devotion. But even these achievements came with a cost. The cathedrals were staggeringly expensive, and the money to build them was often squeezed from ordinary people through taxes and fees.

The universities produced brilliant minds, but their theology sometimes became so abstract and technical that it had little to do with the everyday faith of common believers. The church was reaching for the sky, but many of the people on the ground were being left behind.

A SONG TO LADY POVERTY

Into this world of power, wealth, and spectacle walked one of the most unlikely figures in Christian history: a young man from the Italian town of Assisi named Francis.

Francis (1182–1226) was the son of a wealthy cloth merchant. His father wanted him to become a knight, and Francis spent his early years chasing the glory of military service. But a period of illness and a series of vivid spiritual experiences changed the direction of his life. Francis became convinced that Jesus was calling him to give up everything and live in absolute simplicity, just as the apostles had.

So Francis did exactly that. He gave away his wealth, put on a ragged cloak, tied a rope around his waist, and began wandering the countryside, begging for food and preaching the gospel. He cared for lepers, the outcasts of medieval society. He called his small band of followers the "Lesser Brothers" because they were to be the servants of everyone, not the rulers of anyone. When he came before Pope Innocent III to ask for approval, the contrast could not have been sharper: the most powerful man in Europe, draped in jewels and silk, face to face with a barefoot beggar who claimed to follow Jesus more faithfully than the pope did.

Innocent was wise enough to approve Francis' little order rather than make an enemy of him. The Franciscans grew rapidly, spreading across Europe with their message of humility, poverty, and love. Francis himself tried to go to the Holy Land to preach to Muslims rather than fight them. He met the Sultan of Egypt and, though he did not convert him, earned his respect.

Francis died in 1226, and after his death the order he founded gradually became more organized, more wealthy, and more institutional, despite everything he had stood for. But his example remained a powerful rebuke to a church that had wandered far from the simplicity of the gospel. For a brief moment, as one historian wrote, "the Sermon on the Mount became a realized fact."

A KINGDOM OR A FAMILY?

The medieval church at its height was a breathtaking thing. It produced cathedrals that still take your breath away, universities that still educate the world, and thinkers whose ideas are still studied today. It spread Christianity across an entire continent and gave Western civilization many of its foundational institutions.

But it had also become something that would have been unrecognizable to the apostles. The popes wielded political power over nations. The church owned vast estates and collected enormous sums of money. The clergy lived in luxury while many of their people lived in poverty. The Inquisition tortured and executed people who disagreed with official church teaching. The Crusades sent thousands to kill and die in the name of a Savior who had told Peter to put away his sword.

The church looked more like a kingdom than a family. And like Kuzco in his golden palace, it had become so absorbed in its own power that it had forgotten the people it was supposed to serve.

The question that hung in the air, even in the thirteenth century, was whether the church would correct itself or whether something would have to break. In the next chapter, we will meet the men who tried to answer that question before it was too late.

WHAT THIS MEANS FOR US

First, power and service do not mix easily. The medieval church gained enormous political power, and that power changed the way it operated. Churches today may not command armies, but the temptation to pursue influence, prestige, and control is just as real. Jesus said the greatest among his followers would be the servant of all (Mark 10:43–44).

Second, the gospel cannot be spread by force. The Crusades are a permanent reminder that the sword is not God's method for building his kingdom. People come to Christ through love, truth, and the example of changed lives, not through violence or political coercion.

Third, beauty is not a substitute for faithfulness. The Gothic cathedrals were magnificent, but a beautiful building does not guarantee a faithful church. What matters most is not the grandeur of the structure but the truth of the message and the love of the people inside it.

Fourth, simplicity still speaks. Francis of Assisi challenged the most powerful institution in the world with nothing but a ragged cloak and a commitment to the words of Jesus. His example reminds us that the most compelling witness is not wealth or influence but a life that actually looks like the life Jesus described.

TALKING POINTS

1. **Emperor Kuzco had all the power in the world but used it to serve himself. The medieval papacy also accumulated enormous power.** What do you think happens to a person, or an institution, when they have too much power and too little accountability?

2. **The Crusaders believed they were fighting for God, but the results of the Crusades were devastating and often un-Christlike.** Can you think of examples, either historical or modern, where people have done harmful things while believing they were doing God's will? How can we guard against that?

3. **The Gothic cathedrals were built to inspire awe and point people toward God. Some people today believe that impressive church buildings help people worship, while others think the money would be better spent on helping people in need.** What do you think?

4. **Francis of Assisi gave up wealth and comfort to live in poverty and serve others. His example challenged a church that had become obsessed with power and money.** What would it look like today for someone to challenge the church to return to the simplicity of the New Testament?

5. **The medieval church produced both incredible achievements (cathedrals, universities, scholarship) and terrible failures (the Crusades, the Inquisition, political corruption).** How should we think about a period of history

that contains both great good and great evil? Is it possible to appreciate the good without ignoring the bad?

The medieval church had reached for the sky, and for a time it seemed to touch it. But towers built too high eventually crack, and the cracks in the church's foundation were already spreading. In the years ahead, the papacy would be humiliated, corruption would deepen, and voices would rise calling for a return to the Bible alone as the church's authority. Those voices had been whispering for a long time. They were about to start shouting.

Turn the page.

7

VOICES IN THE WILDERNESS

Everyone knows the story of "The Emperor's New Clothes" by Hans Christian Andersen. Two swindlers convince the emperor that they have woven a magnificent suit from a fabric so special that only wise and worthy people can see it. In reality, there is no fabric at all. The emperor puts on the invisible clothes and parades through the streets completely naked. His advisors, his courtiers, and his citizens all pretend to admire his outfit because none of them wants to look foolish. Finally, a small child in the crowd blurts out what everyone can see but nobody will say: "He has nothing on at all!"

By the fourteenth and fifteenth centuries, the medieval church was parading through Europe in invisible clothes. The corruption was visible to anyone willing to look. Popes lived in luxury while their people struggled. Church offices were bought and sold like merchandise. The papacy split in two, then in three, with rival popes excommunicating each other. The gap between what the church claimed to be and what it actually was had become enormous. But most people kept silent, because challenging the church meant risking everything.

A few voices, however, refused to stay quiet. Like that child in the crowd, they pointed at what everyone could see and said it out loud. They paid a terrible price for their honesty, but their words planted seeds that would eventually grow into the Reformation.

A CHURCH IN CRISIS

The problems started at the top. In 1305, the papacy moved from Rome to the city of Avignon in southern France, where it would remain for nearly seventy years. This period became known as the "Babylonian Captivity" of the church, named after the time when the ancient Israelites were held captive in Babylon. During these decades, all the popes were French, and many people across Europe suspected that the papacy had become a tool of the French king. The popes at Avignon gained a reputation for extravagance, heavy taxation, and bureaucracy. They were not the spiritual shepherds that the times demanded.

Then things got worse. In 1378, the church split in what is called the Great Schism. After the papacy returned to Rome, a disputed election produced two rival popes, one in Rome and one back in Avignon. Each pope excommunicated the other and claimed to be the true head of the church. When a council tried to fix the problem in 1409, it only made things worse by electing a third pope. For several years, three men sat on three thrones, each insisting he alone was the rightful successor of Peter.

The spectacle was devastating. Ordinary believers who had been taught that the pope was God's representative on earth now had to choose which of three popes to believe. The credibility of the papacy was shattered. A council at Constance finally resolved the mess in 1417 by removing all three popes and electing a new one, but the damage had been done. The church had shown the world that its leadership was driven more by politics and ambition than by faith.

Meanwhile, corruption ran deep through every level of the institution. The practice of simony—the buying and selling of church positions—was widespread. A man could become a bishop, not because he was qualified to lead, but because he could afford the price. Many clergy were poorly educated and spiritually negligent. Monasteries that had once been centers of devotion and learning had grown wealthy and lazy. And the church continued to extract money from ordinary people through taxes, fees, and the sale of indulgences, documents that promised forgiveness of sins in exchange for cash.

JOHN WYCLIFFE: THE MORNING STAR

The first major voice to cry out against this corruption came from England. John Wycliffe (c. 1330–1384) was a brilliant scholar at Oxford University, one of the most respected minds of his generation. But Wycliffe was more than an academic. He was a man who read his Bible and could not reconcile what he found there with what he saw in the church around him.

Wycliffe attacked the papacy head-on. He argued that Christ, not the pope, was the true head of the church. He condemned the wealth and political power of the clergy, insisting that church leaders should follow the example of Peter and the apostles, who owned nothing. He wrote that "Christ is truth; the pope is the principle of falsehood. Christ lived in poverty; the pope labors for worldly magnificence."

Even more radically, Wycliffe insisted that the Bible, not the pope or church tradition, was the ultimate authority for Christians. He wrote, "The New Testament is of full authority, and open to the understanding of simple men, as to the points that be most needful to salvation." This was a revolutionary idea in an age when the Bible was available only in Latin and only the clergy were supposed to interpret it.

To put his belief into action, Wycliffe led an effort to translate the Bible into English for the first time. He wanted ordinary farmers, craftsmen, and merchants to be able to read God's word for themselves, without depending on a priest to tell them what it said. He also trained and sent out lay preachers, known as Lollards, who traveled the countryside in simple clothing, preaching from the Scriptures in the language of the common people.

The church was furious. Pope Gregory XI condemned Wycliffe's teachings in 1377. But Wycliffe had powerful friends in the English government who protected him, partly because England was at war with France and had no interest in obeying a pope who seemed to be under French influence. Wycliffe continued to write and preach until his health failed, and he died of a stroke in 1384.

But the church was not finished with him. Decades after his death, the Council of Constance declared Wycliffe a heretic, ordered his books burned, and commanded that his bones be dug up from their grave, burned to ashes, and thrown into a river. They did exactly that in 1428, forty-four years after his death. A later writer observed that just as the river carried Wycliffe's ashes to the sea, so his teachings had been carried across the world. Wycliffe's followers gave him a fitting title: the Morning Star of the Reformation.

JAN HUS: THE BOHEMIAN FLAME

Wycliffe's ideas did not die with him. They traveled across Europe, carried by students and scholars, and took root especially in Bohemia (the modern-day Czech Republic). There they found a champion in Jan Hus (c. 1369–1415), a professor and preacher at the University of Prague.

Hus was deeply influenced by Wycliffe's writings. Like Wycliffe, he believed that Christ, not the pope, was the true head of the church. Like Wycliffe, he insisted that the Bible was the final authority for faith and life. And like Wycliffe, he was disgusted by the corruption he saw in the church around him, from the sale of indulgences to the immoral behavior of the clergy.

But Hus was not simply copying Wycliffe. He was a gifted preacher in his own right who attracted enormous crowds at the Bethlehem Chapel in Prague, where he preached in the common language rather than in Latin. He became a beloved figure in Bohemia, a national hero who represented the desire of ordinary people for a purer, simpler Christianity.

Hus also championed a specific practice that became a symbol of his movement: he insisted that ordinary believers should be allowed to receive both the bread and the cup during communion. In the medieval church, the cup was reserved for the clergy alone. Laypeople received only the bread. Hus argued that this practice had no basis in Scripture and that all believers should share in the full meal that Jesus had instituted.

It seemed like a small point, but it touched on a much bigger question: who was the church really for?

The pope excommunicated Hus in 1411. In 1414, the Council of Constance invited him to come and present his views, promising him safe conduct. Hus agreed, believing he would have a fair hearing. He was wrong. Shortly after arriving, he was arrested and thrown into a dungeon. The council had no intention of listening to him. They intended to silence him.

For months Hus was imprisoned in miserable conditions. He was given a trial of sorts, but it was designed to produce a conviction, not a fair hearing. The council demanded that he recant his teachings. Hus refused. "God is my witness," he said, "that the evidence against me is false. I have never thought nor preached except with the one intention of winning men, if possible, from their sins. In the truth of the gospel I have written, taught, and preached; today I will gladly die."

On July 6, 1415, Jan Hus was burned at the stake. His ashes were thrown into the Rhine River. He was forty-five years old.

SEEDS THAT WOULD NOT DIE

The deaths of Wycliffe and Hus did not end their movements. Wycliffe's Lollards continued to spread his ideas underground in England for over a century. In Bohemia, Hus' followers erupted in a fierce rebellion against both the Roman church and the German empire. They fought a series of wars and eventually formed their own independent church, the Unity of the Brotherhood, which survived until the Reformation and beyond.

The ideas these men championed were remarkably similar to what the Reformers would teach a century later: the Bible as the final authority, Christ as the only head of the church, salvation through faith rather than through the rituals of a corrupt institution, and the right of ordinary people to read Scripture in their own language. Wycliffe and Hus were ahead of their time. They saw the problems clearly, but the church was not ready to listen.

One more development was quietly preparing the way for the changes ahead. Around 1440, a German craftsman named Johannes Gutenberg developed a system of movable type that made it possible to print books quickly and cheaply. Before Gutenberg, every copy of the Bible had to be written by hand, a process that took months and produced books only the wealthy could afford. After Gutenberg, books could be produced by the hundreds and eventually by the thousands. When the Reformation finally arrived, the printing press would carry its message across Europe with a speed that no pope or council could contain.

The stage was set. The corruption was undeniable. The ideas were in the air. The technology was ready. All that was needed was a spark. That spark would come from an unlikely source: a troubled monk in a small German university town, armed with a hammer, a sheet of paper, and ninety-five arguments.

WHAT THIS MEANS FOR US

First, the truth needs to be spoken, even when it is dangerous. Wycliffe and Hus spoke up when staying silent would have been much safer. They paid a heavy price, but their courage opened the door for changes that would transform the church. Speaking the truth in love is never easy, but it is always necessary.

Second, the Bible belongs to everyone. Wycliffe's insistence that ordinary people should be able to read the Bible in their own language was revolutionary. We should never take for granted the fact that we can open a Bible anytime we want. That access was purchased at a high cost.

Third, corruption does not fix itself. The medieval church had centuries to reform from within and failed to do so. When leaders refuse to listen, when institutions protect their power instead of pursuing the truth, the problems only grow worse. Accountability and humility are essential for any organization that claims to serve God.

Fourth, one voice can change history. Wycliffe and Hus were not kings or generals. They were a professor and a preacher. But their willingness to stand on the authority of Scripture and challenge a corrupt system planted seeds that grew into the Reformation. You do not have to be powerful to make a difference. You just have to be faithful.

TALKING POINTS

1. **In "The Emperor's New Clothes," everyone could see the truth but only one person was willing to say it out loud. Wycliffe and Hus were like that person.** Why do you think it is so hard for people to speak up when they see something wrong, especially when the institution they are challenging is powerful?

2. **Wycliffe believed that the Bible should be translated into the language of ordinary people so that everyone could read it for themselves. The church at the time believed only trained clergy should interpret Scripture.** What do you think

are the benefits and the responsibilities that come with having the Bible in your own language?

3. **Jan Hus was promised safe conduct to the Council of Constance but was arrested and burned at the stake instead. The council believed that promises made to a heretic did not have to be kept.** What does this tell you about the state of the church at that time? How important is it to keep your word, even to people you disagree with?

4. **The Great Schism gave the church three rival popes at the same time, each claiming to be the true leader of the church. Imagine you were a regular Christian living during that period.** How do you think that experience would have affected your faith in the church's leadership?

5. **Gutenberg's printing press made it possible for books, including the Bible, to be produced quickly and cheaply for the first time. Technology changed the way people received information then, and it continues to do so today.** How has technology changed the way you learn about the Bible and your faith?

The voices in the wilderness had been silenced, at least for the moment. Wycliffe was dead and his bones scattered. Hus was ashes in the Rhine. The church had survived their challenges and returned to business as usual. But it had not answered their questions. The Bible was still locked away in Latin. The pope still claimed absolute authority. Indulgences were still for sale. And in 1483, in the German mining town of Eisleben, a baby boy named Martin was born to a man named Hans Luther.

Turn the page.

8

HERE I STAND

You probably know what it feels like. Maybe a teacher accuses you of something you did not do, and the whole class is watching. Maybe a group of friends is pressuring you to go along with something you know is wrong, and you are the only one who objects. Maybe a coach or an authority figure tells you to take back something you said, and you know in your gut that what you said was true.

In that moment, everything inside you is pulling in two directions. One voice says, "Just back down. It is not worth the trouble. Say what they want to hear and move on." The other voice says, "If you give in now, you will lose something you cannot get back."

Nearly everyone faces that moment at some point. But very few people have faced it on the scale that a German monk named Martin Luther faced it in the spring of 1521. Luther stood in a packed hall before the most powerful ruler in Europe, surrounded by princes, bishops, and officials of the Roman church, and was given one simple command: take it back. Deny what you have written. Submit to the authority of the pope and the church. Do it now, or face the consequences.

What Luther said next split the Western church in two and changed the course of history.

A MONK WHO COULD NOT FIND PEACE

Martin Luther was born in 1483 in the German mining town of Eisleben. His father, Hans, was a hardworking man who scraped his way from poverty into the middle class and wanted his son to become a lawyer. Martin was bright and obedient, and he enrolled in law school at the University of Erfurt.

But in July 1505, everything changed. While walking near the village of Stotternheim, Luther was caught in a violent thunderstorm. A bolt of lightning struck the ground near him, throwing him to the dirt. Terrified, he cried out a vow: if God would spare his life, he would become a monk. Two weeks later, much to his father's anger, he entered an Augustinian monastery.

Luther threw himself into monastic life with an intensity that alarmed even his superiors. He fasted for days, prayed for hours, confessed every sin he could think of, and punished his body in search of spiritual peace. But peace would not come. No matter how hard he tried, Luther could not escape the feeling that he was a guilty sinner standing before a righteous God. He later wrote, "If ever a monk got to heaven by his sheer monkery, it was I. If I had kept on any longer, I should have killed myself."

The breakthrough came through the Bible. Luther was assigned to teach Scripture at the new University of Wittenberg, and as he studied the book of Romans, one verse seized him: "The just shall live by faith" (Romans 1:17). Slowly, a revolutionary idea took shape in his mind. Salvation was not something you earned through good works, religious rituals, or the approval of priests. It was a gift from God, received through faith in what Christ had already done. Luther later described the moment: "Thereupon I felt myself to be reborn and to have gone through open doors into paradise."

This discovery would change everything. If salvation comes through faith in Christ, then the entire system of the medieval church—built on earning God's favor through sacraments, penances, pilgrimages, and payments—was built on a foundation that Scripture did not support.

NINETY-FIVE SPARKS

The event that lit the fuse was the sale of indulgences. An indulgence was a document issued by the church that promised forgiveness of sins, either for the buyer or for a dead loved one believed to be suffering in purgatory. The practice had been around for centuries, but by Luther's day it had become a shameless money-making operation.

In 1517, a traveling preacher named Johann Tetzel was selling indulgences across Germany to raise money for the construction of St. Peter's Basilica in Rome. Tetzel's sales pitch was as crude as it was effective: "As soon as the coin in the coffer rings, the soul from purgatory springs." Ordinary people, desperate to help their dead relatives, handed over money they could barely afford in exchange for a piece of paper that promised heavenly relief.

Luther was horrified. He saw people in his own congregation waving their indulgence certificates and believing they no longer needed to repent of their sins. On October 31, 1517, following the custom of the university, he posted ninety-five points for debate on the door of the Castle Church in Wittenberg. The theses argued that indulgences could not remove guilt, that true repentance was a matter of the heart, and that the pope had no authority over purgatory.

Luther intended to start an academic discussion. What he got was an explosion. Thanks to the recently invented printing press, copies of the ninety-five theses spread across Germany in a matter of weeks. Within months, they had reached every corner of Europe. Luther had touched a nerve. Millions of people who had been quietly frustrated with the church's corruption suddenly had a voice.

THE POINT OF NO RETURN

At first, Luther did not intend to break with the church. He considered himself a faithful son of Rome who was simply pointing out abuses that needed correction. But the pope saw things differently. In 1520, Pope Leo X issued a formal document condemning forty-one of Luther's teachings and giving him sixty days to take them back or face excommunication.

Luther's response was unforgettable. He led a crowd of students outside the walls of Wittenberg and burned the pope's document in a bonfire. "They have burned my books," he said. "I burn theirs." There was no going back.

In April 1521, Luther was summoned to appear before the Diet of Worms, a formal assembly of the rulers and officials of the Holy Roman Empire, presided over by Emperor Charles V. Luther was shown a table piled with his own books and asked two questions: Did he acknowledge that these were his writings? And would he recant what he had written?

Luther confirmed the books were his. Then he asked for time to consider the second question. The next day he returned and delivered the most famous words of the Reformation: "Unless I am convicted by Scripture and plain reason, I do not accept the authority of popes and councils, for they have contradicted each other. My conscience is captive to the Word of God. I cannot and I will not recant anything, for to go against conscience is neither right nor safe. Here I stand. I can do no other. God help me."

The emperor declared Luther an outlaw. Anyone could kill him without legal consequence. But Luther's protector, Frederick the Wise of Saxony, had him kidnapped on the road home and hidden in a remote castle called the Wartburg. There, in hiding, Luther began translating the New Testament into German so that ordinary people could read God's word for themselves.

WHAT LUTHER CHANGED

When Luther emerged from hiding, the Reformation was already sweeping across Germany. Town after town abandoned the old ways and adopted the new. Luther's reforms touched every part of church life.

He abolished the office of bishop, arguing that the New Testament called for shepherds, not rulers. He insisted that ministers should be allowed to marry, and he himself married a former nun named Katharina von Bora. He revised the worship service, translating it from Latin into German so that the congregation could understand and participate. He restored the practice of giving the communion cup to all believers, not just the clergy. And above all, he placed the Bible at the center of everything, translating the entire Scripture into German in a version so beautifully written that it helped shape the German language itself.

Luther's core convictions can be summarized in three phrases that became the rallying cries of the Reformation. Scripture alone: the Bible, not the pope or church tradition, is the final authority. Faith alone: salvation comes through trusting in Christ, not through earning God's favor by good works. Grace alone: salvation is a free gift from God, not something humans can achieve on their own.

WHERE THE REFORM STOPPED SHORT

Luther's contribution to Christianity was enormous. He broke the stranglehold of the papacy, returned the Bible to the people, and recovered the New Testament teaching that salvation is by God's grace through faith. But Luther was a man of his time, and his reform did not go as far as the New Testament itself would suggest.

Luther retained the practice of infant baptism, even though the New Testament pattern connects baptism with personal faith and repentance. He maintained a close alliance between the church and the state, allowing German princes to control the churches in their territories. And while he rejected the Catholic doctrine that the bread and wine of communion literally become the body and blood of Christ, he still insisted that Christ's body was physically present "in, with, and under" the bread and wine, a view that put him at odds with other Reformers.

In Switzerland, a contemporary named Huldreich Zwingli was leading a parallel but independent Reformation. Zwingli agreed with Luther on many points but went further in some areas, particularly on the Lord's Supper. Zwingli argued that the bread and wine were symbols, a remembrance of Christ's sacrifice, not a physical presence. The two men met at Marburg in 1529 to try to resolve their differences, but they could not agree. The Reformation was already fragmenting into competing movements, each claiming to follow Scripture but arriving at different conclusions.

Luther died in 1546, having transformed Western Christianity. He was not a perfect man. In his later years, he could be harsh, stubborn, and intolerant of those who disagreed with him. But his central achievement remains: he pointed millions of people back to the Bible and to the simple gospel that salvation is a gift of God's grace.

WHAT THIS MEANS FOR US

First, one person's courage can change the world. Luther was a single monk at a small university in an unimportant German town. But because he refused to back down from what he believed the Bible taught, he changed the course of history. You do not need to be powerful to make a difference. You need to be faithful.

Second, the Bible must be the final authority. Luther's great insight was that popes, councils, and traditions can all be wrong. Only Scripture is the unchanging word of God. When human teachings and biblical teaching conflict, the Bible wins.

Third, salvation is a gift, not a paycheck. The medieval church had turned salvation into a transaction: do enough good works, buy enough indulgences, obey enough rules, and you earn your way to heaven. Luther recovered the New Testament truth that salvation is a free gift of God's grace, received through faith in Christ. We cannot earn what God freely gives.

Fourth, reformation is an ongoing task. Luther made enormous progress, but he did not finish the job. His reform still carried elements that went beyond or fell short of the New Testament pattern. The call to return to Scripture is not a one-time event. Every generation must measure its beliefs and practices against God's word.

TALKING POINTS

1. **The chapter opened with the experience of being pressured to back down from something you know is true. Luther faced that pressure at the Diet of Worms and refused to give in.** Can you think of a time when you had to stand your ground on something, even though it would have been easier to stay quiet?

2. **Luther spent years in a monastery trying to earn God's approval through fasting, prayer, and self-punishment, but he never found peace. He finally found it when he realized that salvation is a free gift received through faith.** Why do you think so many people still struggle with the idea that they cannot earn God's love?

3. **The sale of indulgences took advantage of ordinary people's love for their families and their fear of death. Tetzel promised that a payment could free a loved one from**

suffering in purgatory. What made this practice so harmful, and what does it reveal about the state of the church at that time?

4. **Luther translated the Bible into German so that ordinary people could read it for themselves. Before that, most people depended entirely on the clergy to tell them what God's word said.** How might your faith be different if you could not read the Bible on your own?

5. **Luther's Reformation made enormous progress but did not fully return to the New Testament pattern in every area. He kept infant baptism, maintained close ties between church and state, and disagreed with other Reformers about the Lord's Supper.** Why do you think it is so hard for any reform movement to go all the way back to the original?

Luther had struck the first blow. The pope's authority was broken in much of Europe, and the Bible was in the hands of the people for the first time in centuries. But Luther was not the only Reformer, and his movement was not the only one. In the next chapter, the Reformation ripples outward as new leaders, new ideas, and new movements reshape the map of Christianity.

Turn the page.

9

THE REFORMATION RIPPLES OUTWARD

When Ralph smashes his way out of his own video game in the 2012 film *Wreck-It Ralph*, he thinks he is only changing his own story. He is tired of being the villain, and he wants to prove he can be a hero. But Ralph's rebellion does not just affect his game. It sends shockwaves through the entire arcade. Characters in other games are displaced. New threats emerge. A whole world he never knew existed (the candy-coated Sugar Rush) gets pulled into the chaos. One character's decision to break with the system he was born into changes everything for everyone, in ways nobody could have predicted.

Martin Luther's break with Rome worked the same way. Luther may have started by posting ninety-five theses on a church door in Wittenberg, but the shockwaves did not stop at the German border. Within a generation, the Reformation had spread across Europe, sparking new movements in Switzerland, France, England, Scotland, and the Netherlands. Each movement took the basic Reformation ideas and ran in a different direction. Some went further than Luther ever intended. Others used the upheaval for reasons that had nothing to do with theology. And the Roman Catholic Church, shaken but not destroyed, launched a fierce counterattack to reclaim what it had lost.

This chapter follows the Reformation as it ripples outward from Germany and gives birth to the denominations that still shape Christianity today.

JOHN CALVIN AND THE BIRTH OF PRESBYTERIANISM

If Luther was the fiery preacher who lit the match, John Calvin was the careful architect who built the house. Calvin (1509–1564) was a Frenchman, a generation younger than Luther, and a very different kind of person. Where Luther was emotional and impulsive, Calvin was disciplined and methodical. Where Luther was a monk who found freedom, Calvin was a trained lawyer who brought order.

Calvin's conversion came around 1533, through private study of Scripture. He described it as sudden. Soon afterward he was caught up in the persecution of Protestants in France and forced to flee. While on the run, at just twenty-six years old, he published the first edition of his *Institutes of the Christian Religion*, one of the most important books of the Reformation. It was a systematic explanation of Protestant theology that gave the scattered reform movement an intellectual backbone.

Calvin eventually settled in Geneva, Switzerland, where he spent the rest of his life building what he believed a truly reformed Christian community should look like. He established a form of church government led by elders, wrote a catechism for teaching the faith to young people, founded schools, organized care for the poor, and insisted on strict moral discipline for the entire city. Geneva became a model that Christians from all over Europe came to study and imitate.

Calvin's influence was enormous. Refugees who had fled persecution in their home countries came to Geneva, absorbed his theology and system of church government, and then returned home to plant churches. Calvin's ideas became the foundation of Presbyterianism in Scotland (through his follower John Knox), the Reformed churches of France, Germany, Holland, and Hungary, and eventually Puritanism in England and New England. The Presbyterian form of government, in which churches are led by elected elders rather than bishops or a pope, traces directly back to Calvin's Geneva.

HENRY VIII AND THE CHURCH OF ENGLAND

The Reformation in England followed a very different path. It was not started by a theologian or a preacher. It was started by a king who wanted a divorce.

Henry VIII of England had been married to Catherine of Aragon, but after years of marriage she had not given him a male heir. Henry feared that without a son, England could be plunged back into the civil wars that had torn the country apart before his father took the throne. He wanted the pope to annul his marriage so he could marry Anne Boleyn, but Pope Clement VII refused, partly because Catherine's nephew, the powerful Emperor Charles V, was pressuring him to say no.

Henry's response was breathtaking in its boldness. He broke with Rome entirely. In 1534, Parliament passed the Act of Supremacy, declaring the king, not the pope, to be the head of the Church of England. Monasteries were dissolved and their wealth seized by the crown. The institutional ties between England and Rome were cut.

But Henry's break with Rome was political, not theological. He did not share Luther's passion for justification by faith or Calvin's vision of a reformed church. He considered himself a Catholic in everything except his allegiance to the pope. During his reign, the Church of England remained doctrinally close to Roman Catholicism, just without the pope.

Real theological reform came later, under Henry's son Edward VI, and especially under Queen Elizabeth I, who established the Church of England as a middle way between Roman Catholicism and Protestantism. The Anglican tradition (known in America as the Episcopal Church) traces its roots to this English Reformation. It was born not from a monk's crisis of faith but from a king's desire for a male heir. That mixed origin has shaped Anglicanism ever since, giving it a unique blend of Catholic tradition and Protestant theology.

THE ANABAPTISTS: THE RADICAL REFORMERS

While Luther and Calvin reformed the church from within established institutions, a third group wanted to go much further. The Anabaptists believed that both Luther and Calvin had not gone far enough. They insisted on a complete break from the old system, including the deep ties between church and state that both Luther and Calvin had maintained.

The Anabaptists got their name (which means "re-baptizers") because they rejected infant baptism. They argued that baptism was meaningful only when a person was old enough to make a conscious decision to follow Christ. Since they had all been baptized as infants in the Catholic Church, they were baptized again as believing adults. To their opponents, this was scandalous.

But their convictions went well beyond baptism. The Anabaptists taught the complete separation of church and state. They believed the church should be a voluntary community of committed believers, not a political institution tied to the government. Many of them were pacifists who refused to bear arms. They emphasized simple living, personal faith, and following the example of Jesus in daily life.

The Anabaptists were persecuted by almost everyone: Catholics, Lutherans, and Calvinists alike. They were drowned, burned, and driven from their homes. Their crime, in the eyes of the established churches, was not just theological error but social disruption. In a world where church and state were bound together, rejecting one meant rejecting the other.

Despite the persecution, the movement survived. The Anabaptists are the spiritual ancestors of the modern Mennonites (named after the Dutch leader Menno Simons). Their emphasis on believer's baptism, separation of church and state, and voluntary church membership also influenced the development of Baptist churches, though the historical connection between the two groups is more complicated than a straight line.

THE CATHOLIC COUNTER-REFORMATION

The Roman Catholic Church did not simply sit back and watch as half of Europe slipped away. By the middle of the sixteenth century, it launched its own aggressive response, often called the Counter-Reformation or the Catholic Reformation.

The centerpiece of this effort was the Council of Trent, which met in a series of sessions between 1545 and 1563. The council addressed many of the abuses that had fueled the Reformation. It tightened rules for the training and behavior of clergy, condemned the sale of indulgences, and clarified Catholic doctrine on key issues. But Trent also hardened the lines between Catholic and Protestant. The council firmly rejected the Reformation principles of Scripture alone and faith alone, insisting instead that church tradition carried equal authority with the Bible and that both faith and works were necessary for salvation.

A new religious order, the Jesuits (the Society of Jesus), became the most powerful force of the Counter-Reformation. Founded by Ignatius of Loyola in 1540, the Jesuits were highly educated, fiercely loyal to the pope, and committed to winning back territories and souls that had been lost to Protestantism. They established schools and universities across Europe, sent missionaries to Asia, Africa, and the Americas, and served as advisors to Catholic rulers. Their energy and discipline made them one of the most influential organizations in the history of Christianity.

The Counter-Reformation succeeded in halting the spread of Protestantism in much of southern and eastern Europe. Spain, Italy, Portugal, Poland, and large parts of France remained firmly Catholic. But it could not undo the Reformation itself. Western Christianity was permanently divided.

A FRACTURED FAMILY

By the end of the sixteenth century, the Western church that had been united (at least in theory) under the pope for over a thousand years had splintered into a constellation of competing groups. Lutherans dominated in Germany and Scandinavia. Reformed and Presbyterian churches spread across Switzerland, Scotland, France, and the Netherlands. The Church of England went its own way. Anabaptist communities dotted the landscape of central Europe. And the Roman Catholic Church, reformed and reinvigorated, held firm in the south.

Each of these traditions believed it was following the Bible faithfully. Each claimed to represent true Christianity. And each looked at the others with suspicion or outright hostility. The age of one united Western church was over. The age of denominations had begun.

WHAT THIS MEANS FOR US

First, the same Bible can be read differently. The Reformers all claimed to follow Scripture alone, yet they arrived at very different conclusions on baptism, the Lord's Supper, church government, and the relationship between church and state. This does not mean the Bible is unclear. It means that readers must approach Scripture with humility, honesty, and a willingness to let the text speak for itself rather than reading their own assumptions into it.

Second, motives matter. Some Reformers were driven by a genuine desire to return to New Testament Christianity. Others, like Henry VIII, used the Reformation for personal or political gain. The lesson is timeless: it is possible to do the right thing for the wrong reasons, and the results will eventually show it.

Third, courage under persecution reveals character. The Anabaptists were persecuted by Protestants and Catholics alike, yet they held to their convictions. Their insistence on believer's baptism, voluntary church membership, and the separation of church and state would eventually become widely accepted principles. Sometimes the most unpopular position turns out to be the most biblical one.

Fourth, division is costly. The Reformation recovered vital truths that had been buried under centuries of tradition, and that recovery was necessary. But the fragmentation that followed has been one of Christianity's greatest weaknesses ever since. Jesus prayed that his followers would be one (John 17:21). The multiplication of competing denominations is a reminder of how far we still are from that prayer being answered.

TALKING POINTS

1. **Ralph's rebellion in *Wreck-It Ralph* affected the entire arcade, not just his own game. Luther's break with Rome had a similar ripple effect.** Why do you think one person's decision can have such far-reaching consequences?

2. **Calvin built a disciplined, well-organized church in Geneva that became a model for Presbyterians around the world. Luther's movement was more loosely organized.** What are the strengths and weaknesses of having a highly structured church versus a more flexible one?

3. **Henry VIII broke with Rome for personal and political reasons, not because he had a theological disagreement with the pope.** Does it matter why someone does the right thing, or is the result all that counts? How might Henry's motives have affected the kind of church England ended up with?

4. **The Anabaptists insisted on believer's baptism, separation of church and state, and voluntary church membership. These ideas were considered radical and dangerous in the sixteenth century, but many Christians today take them for granted.** Why do you think these ideas were so threatening at the time?

5. **By the end of the sixteenth century, Western Christianity had fractured into Lutherans, Reformed/Presbyterians, Anglicans, Anabaptists, and Roman Catholics. Each group believed it was following the Bible faithfully.** What do you think it would take for Christians today to move closer to the unity Jesus prayed for?

The Reformation had shattered the old order and scattered the pieces across a continent. But the story was not over. Those pieces were about to be carried across an ocean. In the next chapter, the church arrives in a new world, where an experiment in religious freedom will produce something no one in Europe had ever seen: a nation where the government has no official church at all. And in that environment, with no state church to enforce conformity, a simple question will gain new urgency: what if we went all the way back to the Bible and started over?

Turn the page.

10

A CHURCH IN A NEW WORLD

When Robinson Crusoe washes ashore on a deserted island in Daniel Defoe's famous novel, he has lost almost everything. His ship is wrecked. His crewmates are gone. The world he knew is an ocean away. All he has left is what the sea has given back to him and what he can build with his own hands.

But as Crusoe begins to build a new life, something remarkable happens. Stripped of everything he once took for granted, he is forced to ask himself what he truly needs. Not what is nice to have, not what he was used to, but what is essential. A shelter. Fresh water. Food. And, eventually, a Bible, which he salvages from the wreck and begins to read with fresh eyes. Alone on his island, without anyone telling him what to think or how to worship, Crusoe encounters God's word on its own terms.

Something similar happened when Christianity crossed the Atlantic Ocean and arrived in the New World. In Europe, the church had been tangled up with governments, weighed down by centuries of tradition, and fractured into competing denominations that each claimed to be the true version of Christianity. But in America, many of those old structures did not survive the voyage. The new world forced believers to ask a question that would have been unthinkable in Europe: what if we stripped away all the layers of tradition and simply went back to the Bible?

That question would take more than a century to build into a movement. But this chapter tells the story of how the stage was set.

A PATCHWORK OF CHURCHES

By the time the American colonies were well established in the seventeenth and early eighteenth centuries, the religious landscape looked like a patchwork quilt. Different denominations had claimed different regions, and almost every tradition from Europe had planted itself somewhere in the New World.

The Anglicans (the Church of England) dominated the Southern colonies. Virginia, the Carolinas, and Georgia all had the Anglican church as their officially established religion, supported by taxes and backed by law. Jamestown, the first permanent English settlement, was founded in 1607 as an Anglican colony.

The Congregationalists controlled New England. The Pilgrims, a group of separatists who had broken from the Church of England, landed at Plymouth, Massachusetts, in 1620 and introduced the congregational form of church government, where each local congregation governed itself. A decade later, the Puritans arrived and established the Massachusetts Bay Colony with the same Calvinist theology and congregational structure. Their vision was to build a "wilderness Zion," a model Christian community that would shine as a light to the world. Congregationalism spread across Connecticut, New Hampshire, and Vermont.

The Middle Colonies were the most diverse of all. William Penn, a Quaker who had been persecuted in England, founded Pennsylvania as a haven for his fellow Quakers. The Quakers (also called the Society of Friends) believed that God's Spirit speaks directly to every person and that formal clergy, creeds, and elaborate worship were unnecessary. Penn opened his colony to all comers, and Germans flooded in: Lutherans, Moravians, and members of smaller sects. The Dutch brought the Reformed church to New York. Presbyterians established themselves in New Jersey and Pennsylvania. And in Rhode Island, Roger Williams, a separatist who had been expelled from Massachusetts for his radical ideas, founded one of the first Baptist churches in America and championed the principle of complete religious liberty.

By the eve of the American Revolution, the colonies held Anglicans, Congregationalists, Presbyterians, Baptists, Quakers, Lutherans, Reformed, Roman Catholics, and others, all living side by side. No single denomination could claim the whole country. This diversity would prove to be one of the most important factors in the story of American Christianity.

JOHN WESLEY AND THE RISE OF METHODISM

One of the most significant new denominations to emerge during this period had its roots not in America but in England. John Wesley (1703–1791) was an Anglican minister who experienced a dramatic spiritual awakening in 1738 when, at a small meeting on Aldersgate Street in London, he felt his heart "strangely warmed" as he listened to a reading about faith in Christ. From that moment, Wesley became a tireless evangelist, preaching in open fields, in coal mines, and on street corners to crowds that sometimes numbered in the tens of thousands.

Wesley did not intend to start a new denomination. He saw himself as a reformer within the Church of England. But his emphasis on personal conversion, disciplined Christian living, and small-group accountability (he organized his followers into "classes" and "societies" that met regularly for prayer and encouragement) created a movement that eventually outgrew the boundaries of the Anglican church. Wesley's followers were nicknamed "Methodists" because of the methodical discipline of their spiritual lives.

Methodism crossed the Atlantic with remarkable energy. Traveling preachers, known as circuit riders, carried the Methodist message into the most remote corners of the American frontier. They rode on horseback through forests and across rivers, preaching in barns, cabins, and open fields. Their willingness to go where no one else would go made Methodism one of the fastest-growing movements in early American history. By the time the Methodists formally organized as the Methodist Episcopal Church in 1784, they had already become a powerful force on the American landscape.

THE GREAT AWAKENINGS

The most dramatic religious events in colonial and early American history were the Great Awakenings, massive waves of revival that swept across the colonies and transformed the spiritual landscape.

The First Great Awakening began in the 1720s and reached its peak in the early 1740s. It started quietly among Dutch Reformed churches in New Jersey under the preaching of Theodore Frelinghuysen and spread to the Presbyterians through William and Gilbert Tennent. In New England, the brilliant minister Jonathan Edwards preached with such power that entire towns experienced waves of conversion. Edwards' church in Northampton, Massachusetts, saw roughly three hundred people converted in just six months.

The Awakening exploded across the colonies when George Whitefield, a young English evangelist with a voice that could carry across open fields to crowds of thousands, arrived in 1739. Whitefield preached everywhere, to every denomination and every social class. His dramatic, emotional style was unlike anything most colonists had ever experienced. Tens of thousands were converted. Churches that had grown cold and formal were set on fire with renewed passion.

The Second Great Awakening came at the turn of the nineteenth century, after the Revolution had left American religion in a weakened state. Revival fires broke out across the nation, from the settled towns of New England to the rugged frontier of Kentucky and Tennessee. The most famous gathering was the Cane Ridge camp meeting in Kentucky in 1801, where an estimated twenty-five thousand people came together for days of preaching, prayer, and emotional worship. Presbyterians, Methodists, and Baptists worked side by side in these massive outdoor gatherings.

The Awakenings had lasting effects. They brought hundreds of thousands of people to faith. They fueled the growth of Baptist and Methodist churches especially, which thrived on the frontier. They inspired the founding of colleges, missionary societies, and social reform movements. And they reinforced the idea that faith was a personal matter between an individual and God, not something that could be dictated by a government or a state church.

THE GREAT EXPERIMENT: SEPARATION OF CHURCH AND STATE

Perhaps the most revolutionary idea to emerge from the American experience was the complete separation of church and state. For over a thousand years in Europe, church and government had been bound together. Kings appointed bishops. Governments collected taxes for the church. Citizens were born into the established religion of their country whether they chose it or not.

In America, that system gradually fell apart. The sheer diversity of denominations made a single established church impractical. Baptists and Quakers, who had experienced persecution at the hands of established churches, argued passionately that the government had no business interfering in matters of faith. The revivalists of the Great Awakening reinforced the idea that faith was a voluntary, personal decision, not something that could be compelled by law.

When the Constitution was ratified and the First Amendment was adopted, it included words that would have been unthinkable in Europe: "Congress shall make no law respecting an establishment of religion, or prohibiting the free exercise thereof." For the first time in the history of Western

Christianity, a nation had officially declared that the church would stand on its own, without government support or government control.

This was both a challenge and a gift. Without state support, churches had to win their members through persuasion, not coercion. They had to fund themselves through voluntary giving, not through taxes. But they also gained something priceless: the freedom to follow the Bible wherever it led, without asking a king or a parliament for permission.

TOO MANY CHOICES, ONE BIG QUESTION

By the early 1800s, the American religious landscape was more crowded than ever. Congregationalists, Presbyterians, Baptists, Methodists, Episcopalians, Lutherans, Quakers, Reformed churches, and Roman Catholics all competed for the hearts of a growing nation. Each denomination had its own creed, its own form of government, its own traditions, and its own interpretation of Scripture. Choosing a church was like standing in a market with dozens of vendors, each one insisting that their product was the real thing.

For a growing number of thoughtful believers, this multiplication of denominations raised a troubling question. Jesus had prayed that his followers would be one (John 17:21). Paul had written that there is "one body and one Spirit, one Lord, one faith, one baptism" (Ephesians 4:4–5). Yet here were dozens of competing groups, each claiming the authority of the same Bible, each adding its own creed or confession on top of Scripture. How had the simple faith of the New Testament become so complicated?

The answer, some began to argue, was that every denomination, however well-intentioned, had added layers of human tradition to the gospel. The creeds, the confessions, the elaborate systems of church government, the theological disputes that had generated century after century of division—all of these were human additions to something that God had already made complete. What if, instead of reforming one of the existing denominations, believers simply went back to the New Testament itself and rebuilt the church from scratch?

That question was the spark that would ignite the Restoration Movement in the early years of the nineteenth century. Men like Barton W. Stone, Thomas Campbell, and his son Alexander Campbell began calling for Christians to abandon their denominational labels, set aside their human creeds, and unite on the basis of the Bible alone. "Where the Scriptures speak, we speak," they declared. "Where the Scriptures are silent, we are silent."

The Restoration Movement did not seek to create another denomination. It sought to undo the very concept of denominationalism and return to the simple pattern of the New Testament church: believers united by faith in Christ, obeying the gospel as the apostles taught it, and gathering as the church that Jesus himself had built.

WHAT THIS MEANS FOR US

First, freedom and faith go together. The American experiment proved that Christianity does not need government support to survive. In fact, the church thrives best when it stands on its own, relying on the power of God and his gospel rather than the power of the state.

Second, division is not inevitable. The multiplication of denominations happened because human traditions were added to God's word. If Christians are willing to set aside their creeds, confessions, and traditions and return to the Bible alone, the basis for unity already exists. It is written in the New Testament.

Third, the question still matters. The early Restoration leaders asked, "What if we just went back to the Bible?" That question has not expired. Every generation of Christians must ask whether their beliefs and practices are rooted in Scripture or in human tradition. The answer determines whether we are following Jesus or following something else.

Fourth, the story is not over. This book has traced the church from the death of the apostles to the doorstep of the Restoration Movement. But the story of the church did not end in the early 1800s, and it has not ended today. Every Christian who opens a Bible, obeys the gospel, and gathers with other Christian to worship God in spirit and in truth is writing the next chapter.

TALKING POINTS

1. **Robinson Crusoe had to figure out what he truly needed when he was stripped of everything familiar. The early American church had a similar experience in the New World.** What do you think are the essential elements of the church that Jesus built, and what are the extras that have been added over the centuries?

2. **The First Amendment separated church and state for the first time in Western history. Some people believe this**

was the best thing that ever happened to American Christianity because it forced churches to rely on persuasion rather than power. Others worry that it weakened the church's influence. What do you think?

3. **The Great Awakenings brought thousands of people to faith through emotional, personal experiences of conversion. Some people were uncomfortable with this approach and preferred a quieter, more intellectual kind of faith.** What role do you think emotion should play in a person's relationship with God?

4. **By the early 1800s, there were so many denominations that thoughtful Christians began asking whether the whole system had gone wrong. The Restoration leaders proposed going back to the Bible alone, with no human creeds.** What do you think are the biggest obstacles to Christians today uniting around the Bible rather than around denominational traditions?

5. **This book has covered nearly eighteen hundred years of church history, from the death of the apostles to the beginning of the Restoration Movement.** Which chapter, person, or event made the biggest impression on you? Why?

The story of the church is the story of people trying to follow Jesus across the centuries, sometimes faithfully and sometimes not. It is a story of courage under persecution, of truth defended against error, of power gained and abused, of reform attempted and abandoned, and of an ancient question that refuses to go away: what did Jesus actually intend his church to be?

From the simple gatherings described in the book of Acts to the golden cathedrals of the Middle Ages, from the fires that consumed Jan Hus to the printing press that set the Bible free, from the thunderstorms of Luther's Germany to the camp meetings of the American frontier, this story has been heading somewhere. It has been heading back to the beginning.

The Restoration Movement believed that the Bible contains everything the church needs: no more and no less. No pope, no creed, no confession of human invention can improve on what God has already revealed. The call to go back to the New Testament is not a call to live in the past. It is a call to build the future on the only foundation that will last.

The story of the church is still being written. And the next chapter belongs to you.

www.ingramcontent.com/pod-product-compliance
Lightning Source LLC
Chambersburg PA
CBHW051414050726
47595CB00010B/4060